Art from Recycled Materials

Art from

Cheesecloth; block printing inks.

Recycled Materials

Dorothea C. Malcolm

Assistant Professor of Art and Art Education
The William Paterson College of New Jersey

Davis Publications, Inc.
Worcester, Massachusetts

Consulting Editors: George F. Horn, Sarita R. Rainey

Photographs by Howard C. Malcolm

Copyright 1974
Davis Publications, Inc.
Worcester, Massachusetts, U.S.A.

All rights reserved. No part of this publication may be reproduced or transmitted in any form or by any means, electronic or mechanical, including photocopying, recording, or any storage and retrieval system now known or to be invented, except by a reviewer who wishes to quote brief passages in connection with a review written for inclusion in a magazine, newspaper or broadcast.

Printed in the United States of America
Library of Congress Catalog Card Number: 73-93381
ISBN 0-87192-059-x

Printing: The Art Print Co.
Type: 10/11 Melior with Bold
Graphic Design by Repro-Art Service

10 9 8 7 6 5 4 3 2 1

To
William B. Jennison

in recognition of his commitment to sound educational objectives as consistently found in publications he endorsed.

CONTENTS

	INTRODUCTION	9
1.	WOOD	21
2.	LEATHER	37
3.	OTHER MATERIALS FROM NATURE	45
4.	GLASS	52
5.	METAL, WIRE AND FOIL	64
6.	STRINGS AND FABRIC	77
7.	PAPER AND CARDBOARD	92
8.	PLASTICS	110
	ACKNOWLEDGMENTS	127
	BIBLIOGRAPHY	128

INTRODUCTION

Fig. I-1. "Animal Fantasy," 3' × 11', woven recycled woolen skirts. Detail.

Art and the crafts have a long history of recycling: that is, finding merit in cast aside items and using them in new relationships. This wasn't always called recycling, but today we equate the term with our ecological crises.

An awareness of artistic worth in recycling is increasing and people are cooperating with each other in many ways. One example is the involvement of an entire student body in designing and weaving a spectacular three feet by eleven feet woolen mural to commemorate the opening of their new elementary school. The children did not work alone. Mothers

Fig. I-2. Latex outdoor paint on discarded telephone pole.

collected, cleaned and cut discarded, vividly colored woolen pieces into small strips for the youngsters to weave. Fathers built a support and steam-cleaned the finished project. The entire community is justly proud of their "Animal Fantasy" enthusiastically created from scrap.

In another town the Indian culture inspired a third-grade class to fashion totem poles from an old telephone pole donated by the telephone company. After the pole was halved by the school custodian, the children created painted totems, and the finished totems were erected by the telephone company. The group effort resulted in two handsome sentinels guarding the school entrance.

Fig. I-3. Tempera painted cut cardboard packaging shapes.

Fig. I-4   Assorted scrap paper; yarn; balloon.

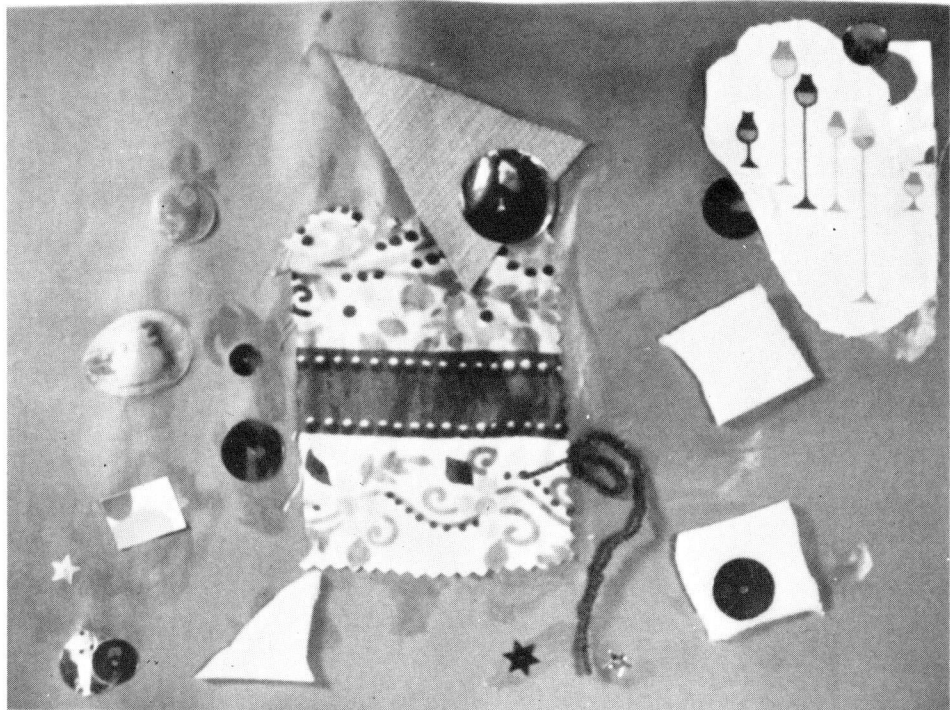

Fig. I-5. Fabric; buttons; seals; wallpaper; yarn.

Common everyday objects found around any home are readily transformed into recycled art forms simply by cutting, painting, gluing and assembling.

Fig. I-6. Glued wood and toothpicks.

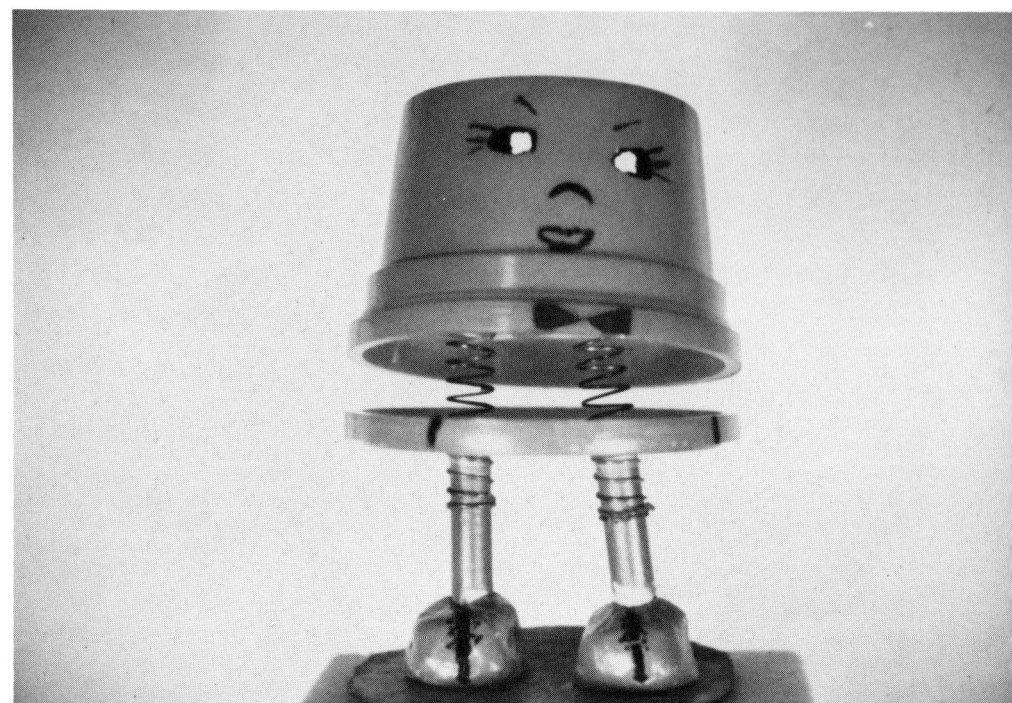

Fig. I-7. Plastic container; dowels; wound wire; clay feet; acrylics.

Fig. I-8. Variety of discarded materials.

Much more can be done in designing with discarded materials using simple tools, such as screwdrivers, pliers or hammers.

Fig. I-9. Shaped plastic pieces; wood; elastic bands; buttons.

Fig. I-10. Discarded buttons mounted on fabric.

It often happens that one collects a number of like, or similar, items which can be converted into recycled art. Arranging them into a pleasing design is always a challenge, because several possibilities must be narrowed down to just one.

17

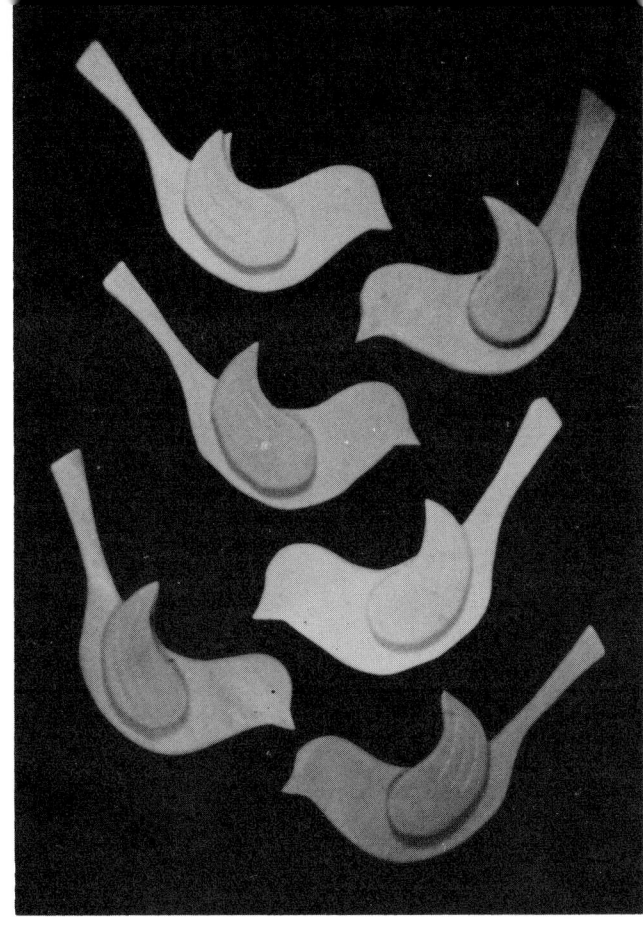

Fig. I-11. Balsa mobile; handmade bird shapes.

Fig. I-12. Paper plates; buttons; straws; felt tip marker.

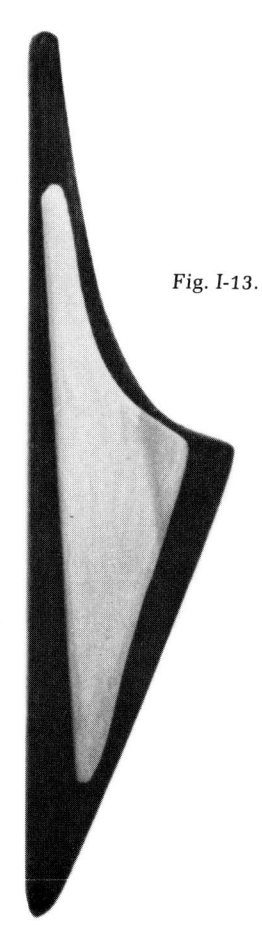

Fig. I-13. Acrylics on scrap pine.

Salvaged metal, wood, plastic and leather are frequently used for personal adornment, such as jewelry, combs, barrettes and buckles. Many are ingeniously made with a minimum of materials and tools.

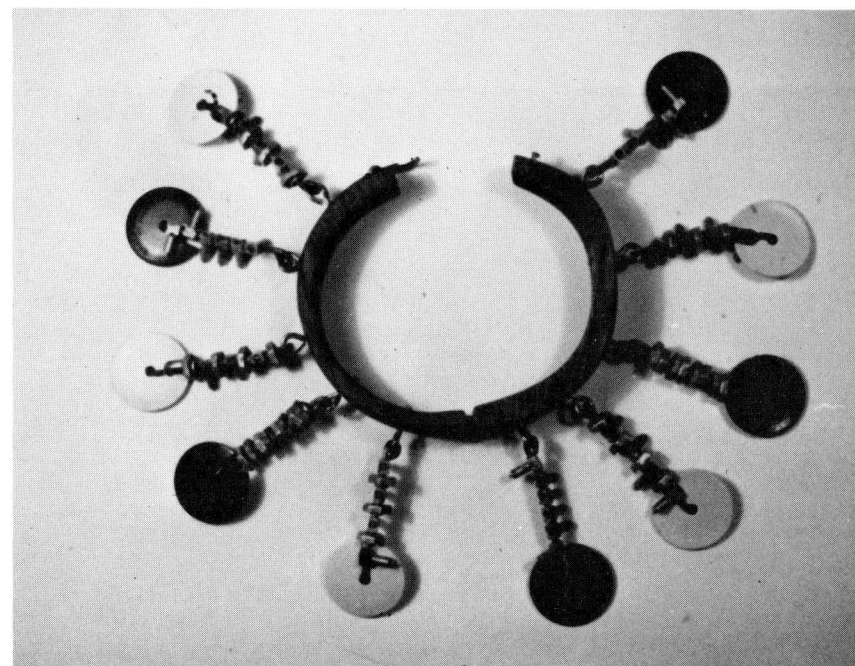

Fig. I-14. Formed wood; metal parts; discs.

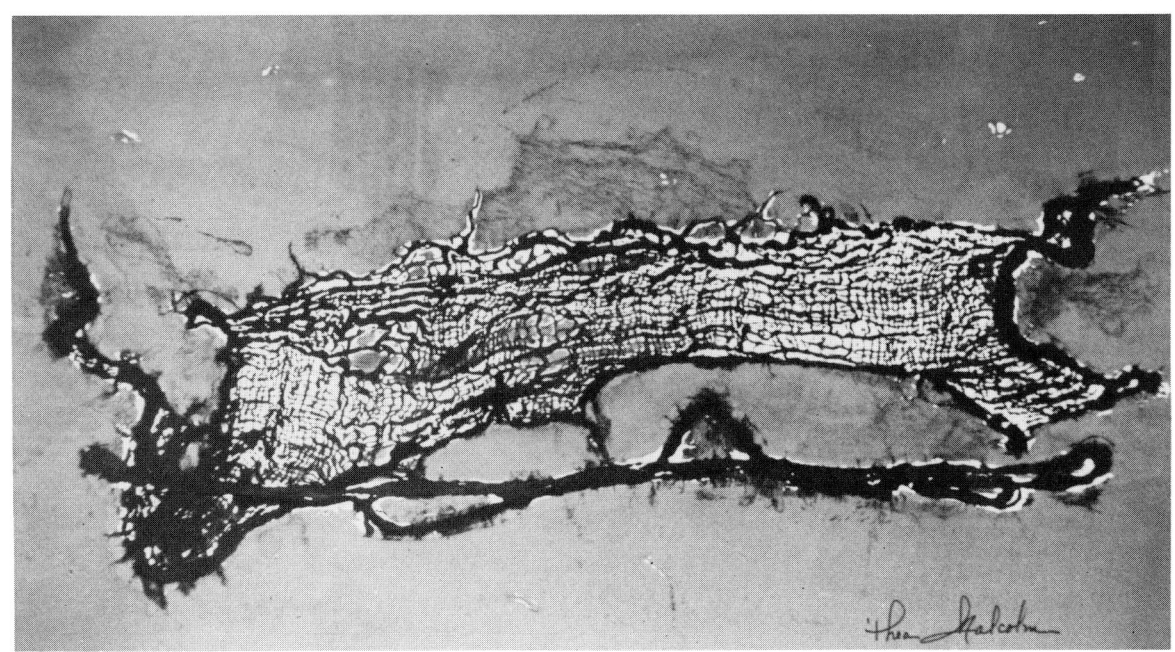

Fig. I-15. Cheesecloth; block printing inks.

Found materials may be impressed on a surface; in Fig. I-15 an odd piece of cheesecloth was used in printmaking. Discarded materials might also be the hidden structure of a design. Styrofoam packaging was cut into forms, then covered with plaster of Paris in Fig. I-16. And some scraps make excellent background surfaces for any art media. See Fig. I-17.

Fig. I-16. *Relief design on wood; 2' × 3'.*

Fig. I-17. *Oil pastel on torn window shade section.*

In countless ways recycling is taking place and there is no way of anticipating what materials you might be called upon to use. This book is written to acquaint you with some of the materials used in recycling and to show you how others have responded to the creative challenges they presented.

Chapter 1
WOOD

Fig. 1-1.

The excitement of recycling begins immediately when you begin looking for wood. You never know exactly what shape, size or type you might find, and seldom have you completely formulated in your mind how the wood will be used.

Green wood is wood that has not had time to dry thoroughly. It is wood gathered from the forest floor or branches picked up in the back yard. A branch might be somewhat flexible, even greenish in color inside, and damp to the touch. Green wood can be used if shrinkage or warpage do not affect the overall design. Taking advantage of their natural growth, the branches in Fig. 1-1 were artfully arranged to give a striking linear effect.

Fig. 1-2.

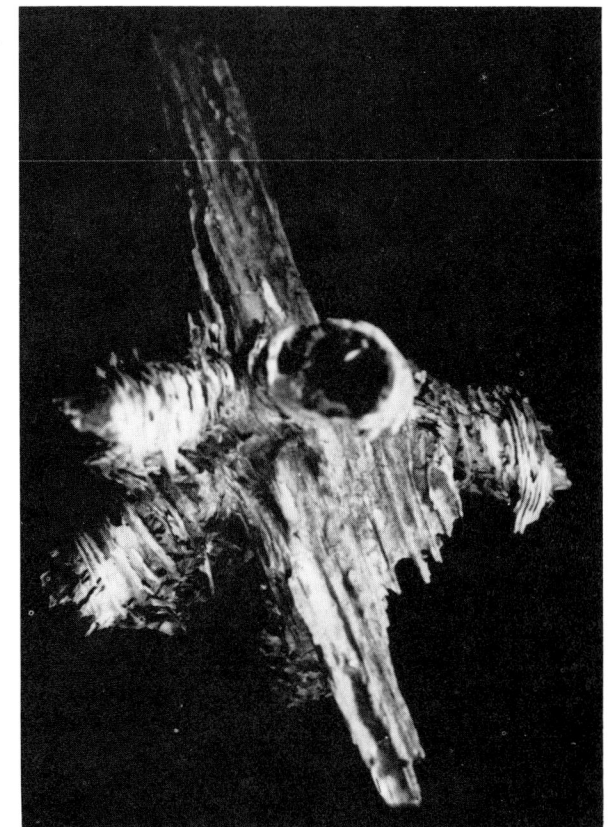

Fig. 1-3.

Exposure to changing weather conditions over a long period of time dried the pine bough seen in Fig. 1-2. It acquired a many-hued, silvery patina impossible to duplicate by artificial means. One might hesitate to change in any manner a branch which has aged so gracefully and beautifully.

However, if found woods do not completely please the craftsman, he can change it in several ways. Sun exposure or chemical bleach lightens the color of the wood. The length of time in a bleach solution and the frequency of immersions depends upon the results sought. This is generally not a very quick process. To darken wood while enriching it rub the surface with boiled linseed oil. If a protective finish is desired but the natural look of wood is to be retained, a light application of furniture or floor wax is used. Wood salvaged from fireplaces or deliberately charred with a torch will have surface as well as color changes. A wire brush will remove unwanted soot and loosen chips of burnt wood.

Nature's discards can bring much pleasure. The natural state of the wood in Fig. 1-3 was altered by washing and brushing it.

Fig. 1-4.

Furniture and wood products manufacturers, cabinet makers, boat builders, woodworking shops, lumber yards, carpenters, wood carvers and sculptors are prime sources of scrap wood. Home or building construction and remodeling sites generally have excess pieces of wood. Many business establishments dispose of all kinds of wood for which they have no use; for example, shipping crates or cartons reinforced with wood. Cellars and attics are particularly good places to find wood; don't overlook community "Clean-Up Week" drives either. Along with odd assortments of wood, there can be found boxes and bowls in all sizes and shapes, picture frames, chairs, tables and other furniture. All or portions of them can be salvaged and used.

After selecting a piece of scrap wood, its best qualities and imperfections should be considered. For example, the wood used in the plaque in Fig. 1-4 has a beautiful grain pattern which would have been lost under a coat of opaque paint. A transparent stain enhanced its character and maintained the integrity of the wood. A knot near the center of the piece might have presented difficulties. Knots are a change in texture or grain; they are extremely hard and are unpredictable when worked on. The design was worked around the knot; it became an acorn.

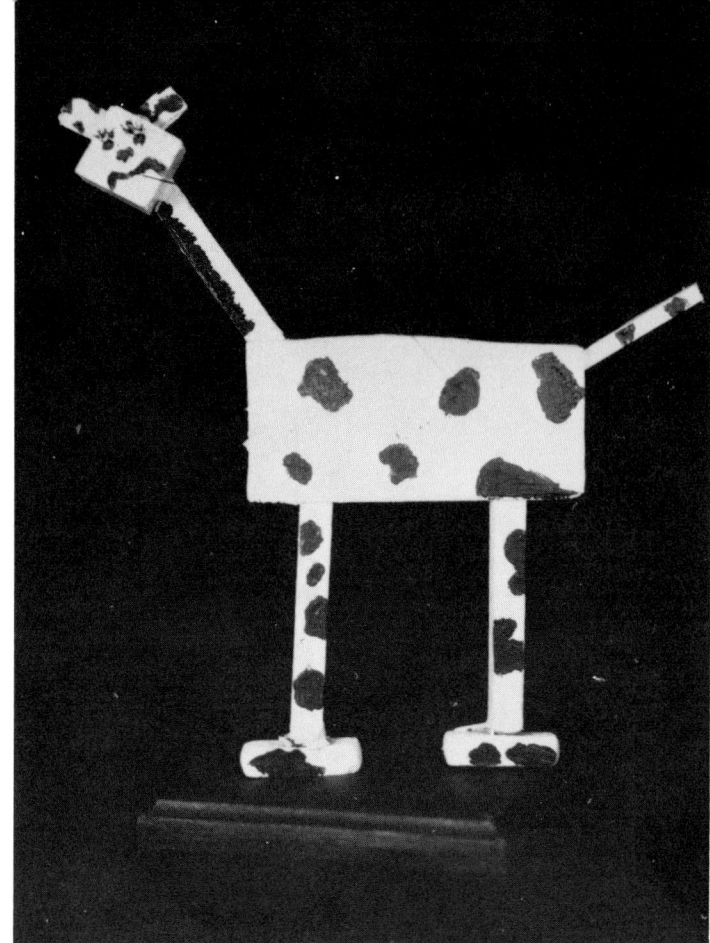

Fig. 1-5. Light sanding, glue and tempera paint.

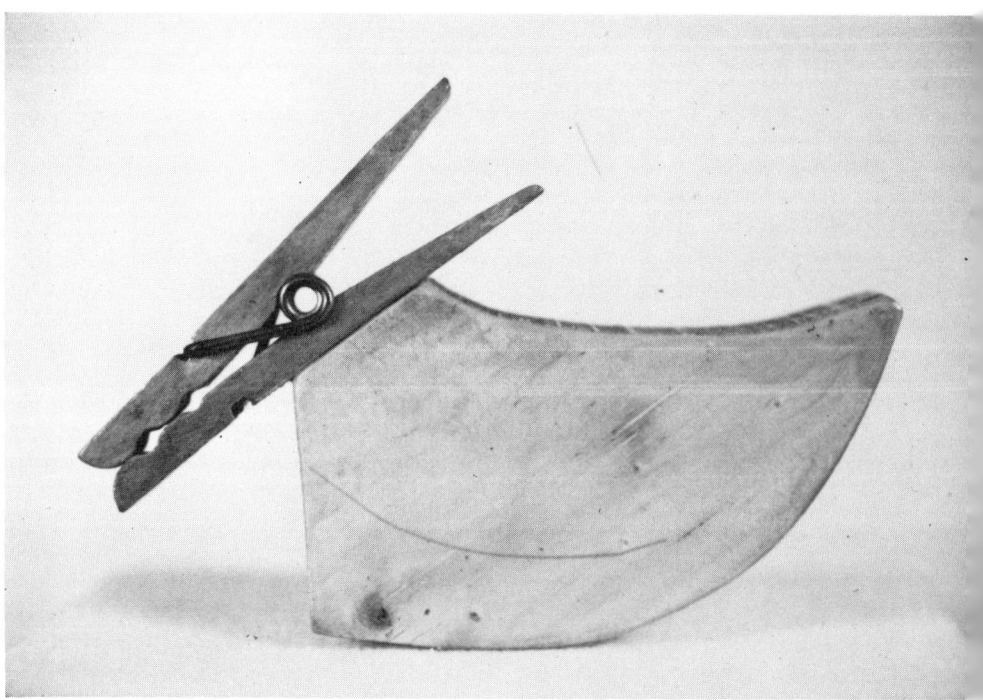

Fig. 1-6. Light sanding, glue and coffee stain.

Fig. 1-7. The wooden disc was sanded smooth, then lightly stained with food coloring. Metal and plastic parts were glued on to make a modern day hex sign.

Upon receiving a basket of scrap pine, a group of children explored ways in which the pieces could be used. There was some independent thinking; others took their cues from class discussion. One boy found three pieces which he insisted could be put together and made into a boat. He wanted glue and paint to make a fine boat, and a long string with which to pull it across the water. Since most of the pieces were somewhat rectangular, one youngster envisioned a town; each child would make a building. Maria was going to glue some of her collection of tiny seashells on her piece of wood and give it to her great aunt who lived near the beach. Some of the children liked her idea. They, too, had collections: marbles, old coins, pebbles, bones, stamps, pods, buttons, assortments of small trinkets. Tom said, "Why do anything?" He liked the pieces just the way they were. Leave them in the basket. Whenever they wanted to, anyone could use them to build or play. A few of the ideas were hardly feasible for classroom work; they were modified to fit within the realm of possibility. Basic materials used were strong coffee for light staining, tempera for those who needed color, glue and shellac for permanence. Glued pieces were dried on waxed paper which did not stick to them as they dried. A piece of gaily colored felt was glued to the bottom of some pieces to prevent marring furniture. Since everyone has different ideas and a unique way of seeing the art possibilities in a given piece of wood, we cannot say that it must be used in only one way. Figures 1-5 through 1-11 are spontaneous responses carried out in a simple, direct manner.

Fig. 1-8. The paint stirrer was painted and strips of slit plastic foam were glued on to make a dust brush.

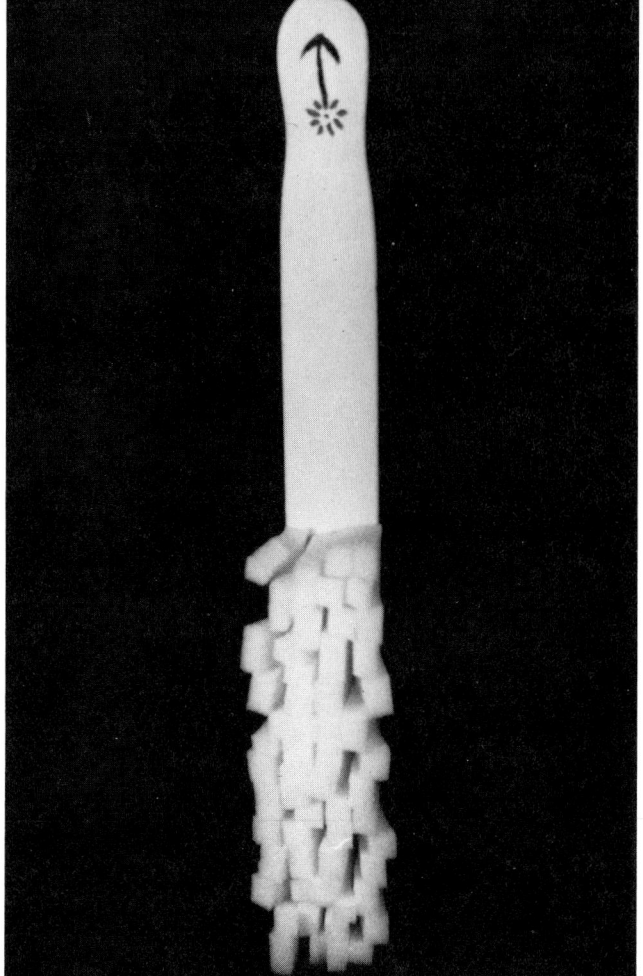

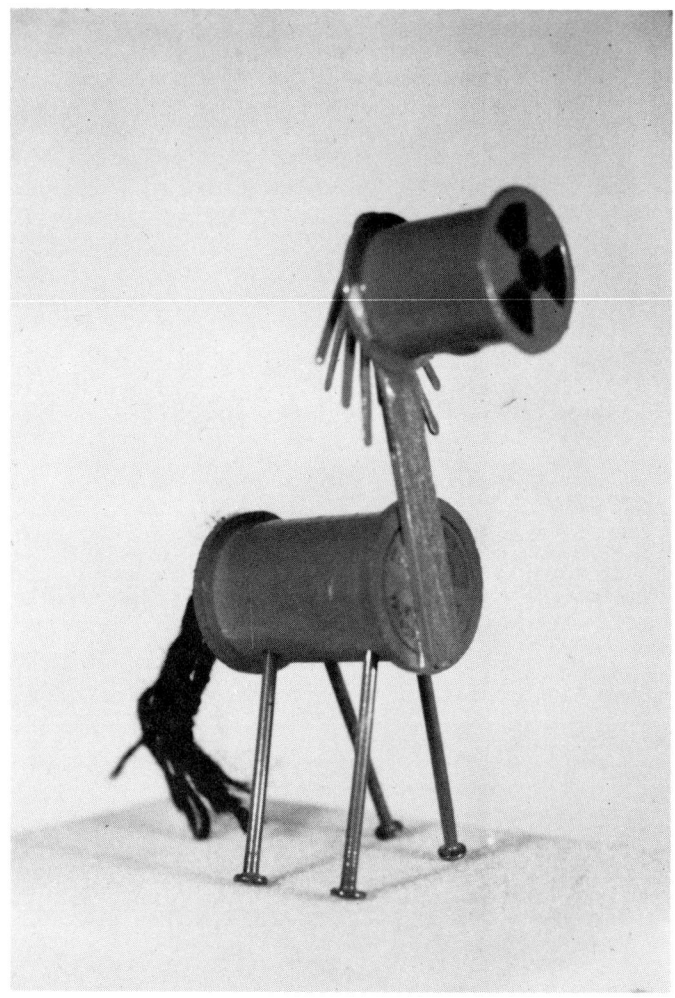

Fig. 1-9. Spools, toothpicks, popsicle stick, nails and yarn were put together and painted to make this whimsical creature.

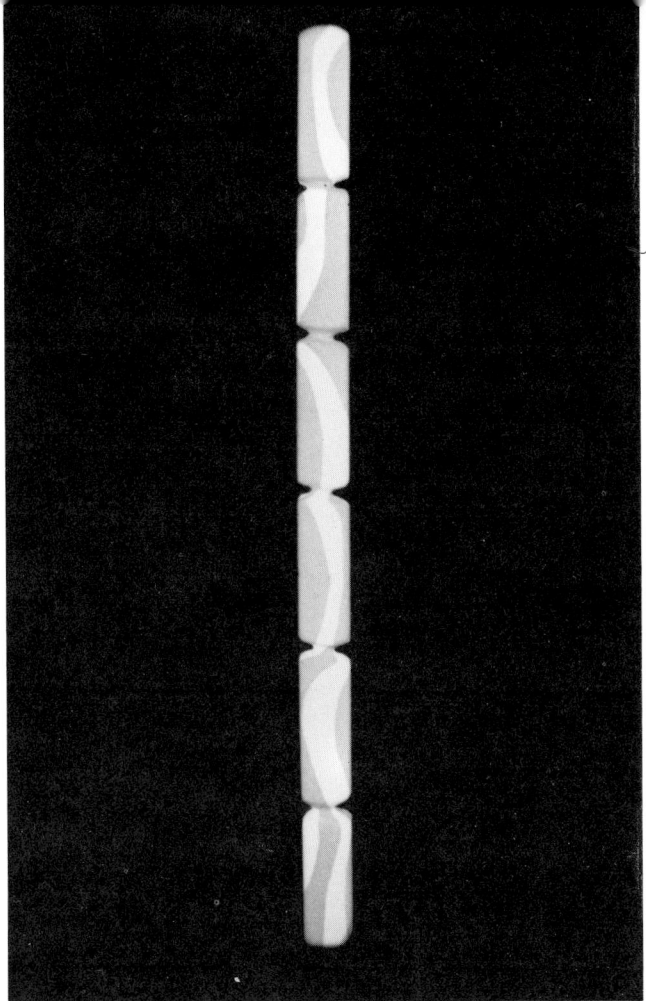

Fig. 1-10. A stick of very soft wood was sanded into a totem form and painted.

Fig. 1-11. The piece of wood was sanded and painted. Odd pieces of scrap wood were glued on to add a three-dimensional quality to the beach scene.

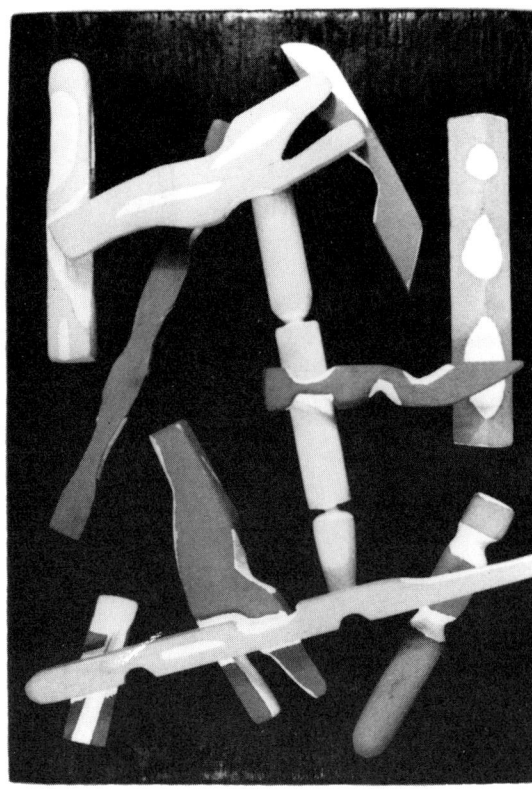

Fig. 1-12. Scrap balsa pieces sanded into forms, painted with acrylics and mounted on salvaged painted pine.

Balsa is familiar to many children. They use it in model making and generally buy it in hobby shops in strips, rods or laminated block forms. Balsa is an extremely soft wood. Wetting and bending strips into a shape is possible. A dent can be made with a fingernail and scissors easily cut the thinner strips. To prevent splitting when cutting or sawing thin balsa, it is a good idea to tape the underside. Sandpaper can also be used for shaping the wood.

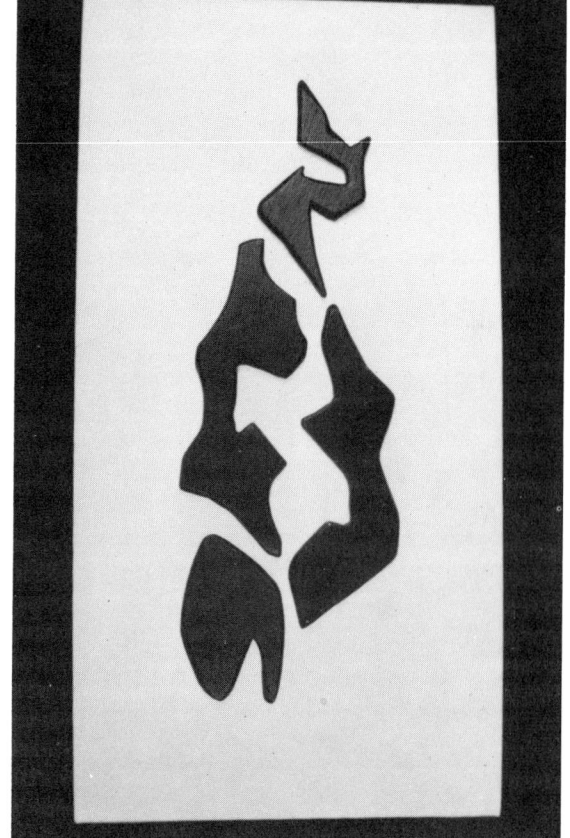

Fig. 1-13. Colored with a permanent felt tip marker; cooking oil rubbed in for a soft sheen.

Fig. 1-14. Tempera; polymer medium for a protective coating; mounted on cork.

Two useful tools when working with wood are rasps and rifflers. They are made in many sizes and have different designs, but the most common ones have pointed little teeth covering their working surfaces to scrape or grate the wood. Some of them comfortably fit a child's hand and are ideally suited for carving in soft wood. The sturdy ones can give years of service. They can also be used on many other materials in addition to wood with satisfying results. The accompanying illustrations show soft wood forms individually created with either rasps or rifflers. They were hand sanded with a fine abrasive before final finishing.

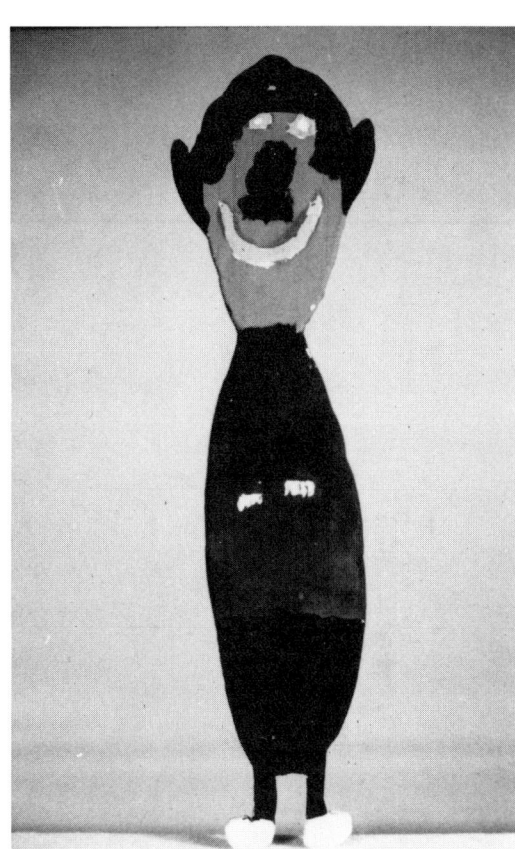

Fig. 1-16. Tempera.

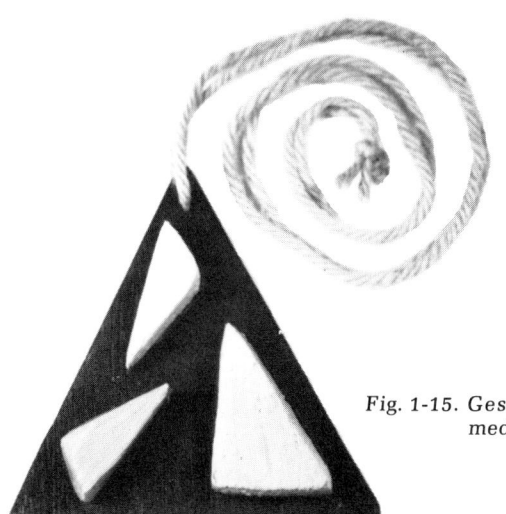

Fig. 1-15. Gesso; water color; polymer medium.

Fig. 1-17. Pine; tempera; shellac.

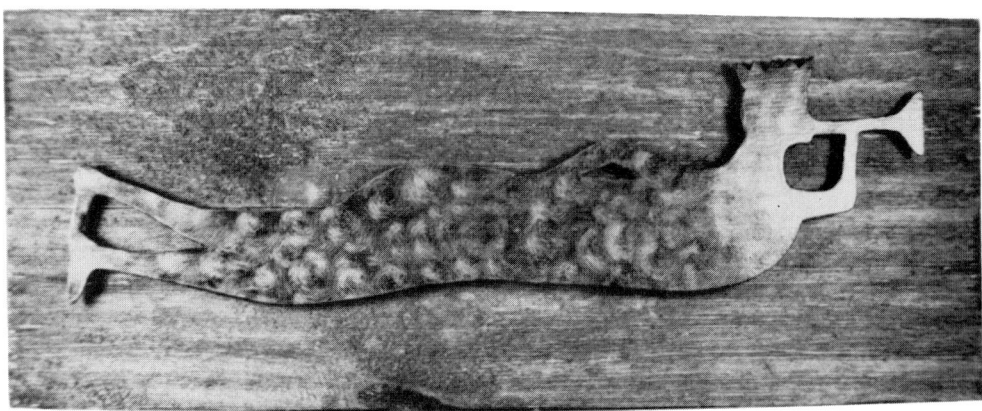

Fig. 1-18. Linden; acrylics; aged wood mounting.

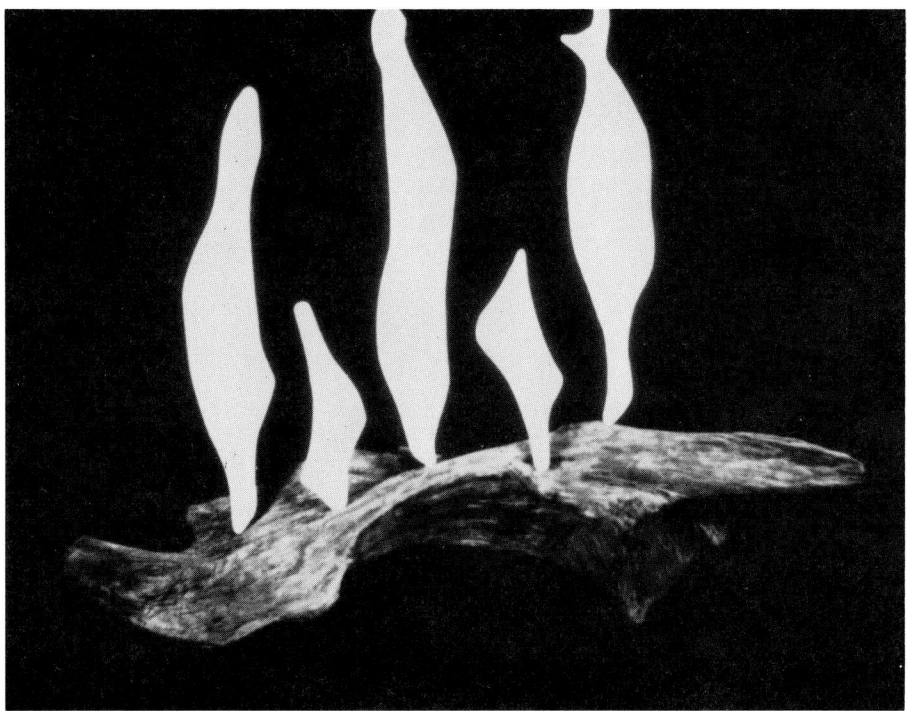

Fig. 1-19. Balsa; tempera; matte polymer medium; mounted on driftwood.

Fig. 1-20. Pine; enamel.

Economy of time and labor often demands a sharper cutting edge. A coping saw is an efficient tool for cutting shapes out of soft wood such as balsa, pine and basswood. The wood must be held firmly when sawing. A convenient way to do this is to make a bench pin. It is simply a piece of wood with a long, slender V notched into it and is either clamped to a sturdy surface or held securely in a vise. The wood to be sawed is clamped to it. The bench pin does two things: it prevents the wood from the chattering that hinders sawing and it permits the saw blade to reach some distance into the wood. Children derive tremendous satisfaction from using a coping saw. At first a little patience is required in using one, but skill comes with practice. Figures 1-17 through 1-20 are examples of figures initially cut out with a coping saw. They were refined with whatever means would accomplish the end results: rasps, rifflers, steel wool, coarse to fine sandpapers.

Fig. 1-21. An interchangeable arrangement.

Some woods offer more resistance and using a regular cross-cut saw is more practical for cutting the wood. In Fig. 1-21 we see four separate pieces of scrap wood which can be arranged in any manner. They were shaped with a saw, sanded and enameled.

Fig. 1-22. Knife marks give texture; stain and acrylics.

There's hardly a boy who hasn't at some time taken his pocket knife to a piece of wood and at least cut shavings or a crude carving. This is whittling. It is called "carrying" or "pocket" art, because the wood is small; it often fits in a pocket and can be carried anywhere to whittle at will. The softer the wood, the less resistance there is to the pressure of a cutting knife. To be sure, there are times when a knife slips or a pocket knife folds in upon itself. That is precisely why whittling is generally not recommended for small children; but an interested adolescent can whittle in earnest.

Fig. 1-23. Carved; tea stained; waxed.

A number of wood surface carvings are best accomplished with knives or single-edged blades. Some older children take pride in being able to do these exacting and somewhat tedious wood carvings. They are not quite as hazardous as whittling, because hands can be kept out of the way of the cutting edge. These requirements must be met: an easy to carve wood with a close and even grain; a well thought out design clearly marked on the wood; and a sharp blade. Discarded pine boxes can be transformed into intricate carvings. In fact, any flat, smoothly-sanded piece of close-grained soft wood can be successfully used.

Fig. 1-24. Light stain and waxed.

Chip carving is a more demanding method of carving. Triangular three-dimensional chips of wood are cut out of the surface with a single-edged blade or a chip carving knife. A jagged cavity should not remain after these wedges are lifted out. The true beauty of chip carving lies in its preciseness. To achieve perfect pyramid-like shapes, three angular cuts meet in the wood underneath the chip. Improvisations appear as control of the knife is mastered; after some experience chisels might be tried.

Fig. 1-25. Detail of chip carving plaque.

Fig. 1-26. Light stain; polyurethane finish.

It is easy to carve into a balsa wood surface with blunt objects, and a deep linear quality can be quickly achieved by using a paper clip or pencil. But other woods are more resistant and require sharper tools to penetrate them. Appropriate tools for carving are chisels, gouges, veiners and various related tools. Only a few good quality tools are needed to insure a carver of rewarding experiences in woodcarving.

Chapter **2**

LEATHER

Primitive societies used leather in practical ways and a few of their members embellished it. For example, some American Indians embroidered leather with dyed porcupine quills or colored beads. Leather has been widely used by man in countless ways throughout the history of civilization, but its demand decreased as manufactured materials replaced it. In an effort to escape our mass-produced synthetics, people are turning to naturally beautiful materials, and leather is among them. Since progress always proceeds in a spiral, today's leathercraft reflects the skills of the past, modern technology and contemporary design.

There was a time, not too long ago, when getting scrap leather depended on knowing a leather craftsman, a saddle or harness maker, or upon living near a shoe factory. These are still good sources and local inquiry might uncover unexpected leather discards. But to make it all very simple, bags of scrap leather are sold through hobby shops, retail stores and school supply dealers. Many of the blemishes on leather are a record of what the animal endured in battles, experienced while roaming the terrain or through branding. They do not affect the quality of the skin. Craftsmen have learned to work around objectionable flaws and to incorporate others into their

Fig. 2-1. Colored inks; stitchery; pocketbook scraps.

designs. They know that most leather, even used shabby-looking leather, can be reclaimed with proper treatment because it is extremely durable and can be used again and again. Leather can be cleaned with soap and water. Applying a leather conditioner will keep it supple. To prevent drying and cracking of the leather the conditioner is applied periodically. Waxing is a protection. Finishing compounds protect against stains and watermarks. An exception is suede. The nap is created by buffing or sanding the skin and requires special care.

In addition to rich earth tones, leather is dyed in a surprising array of pastels and brilliant colors. Commercial leather dyes are available to the novice. Not all leathers take successfully to dyes, especially if they have been coated with a finish. If you are not familiar with the leather you are using, it is still worth experimenting to produce an exciting color. For art forms where wear is not a factor, anything that stains might be successful: colored inks, permanent felt tip markers and pens, thinned acrylic paints, wood and glass stains, coffee, tea and other food colorants. Color absorbency will always differ, even on the same skin. Apply stain very lightly with a small soft cloth to prevent unwanted streaking. Several light applications are better than getting too dark a stain all at once. When the knack of staining is learned, and it doesn't take too long, leather can be mottled, accented and striped. Batik and tie-dye are successful with pliant leathers. Always test-piece suede when staining.

Fig. 2-2. Government surplus: leather and findings.

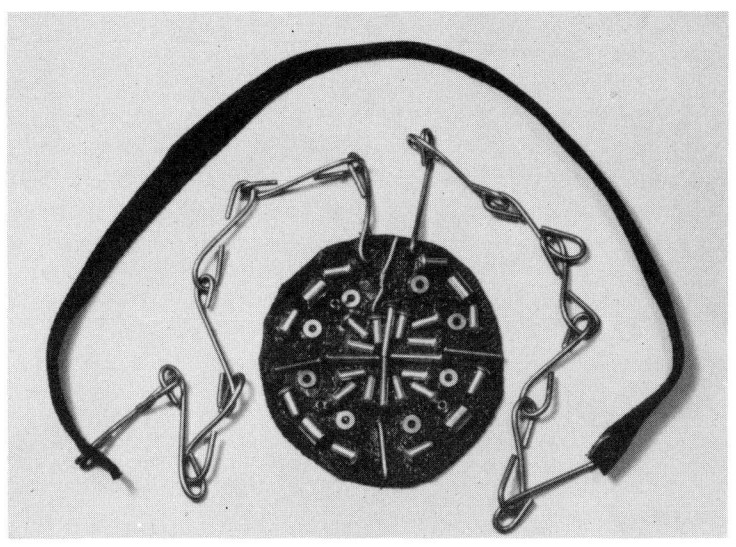

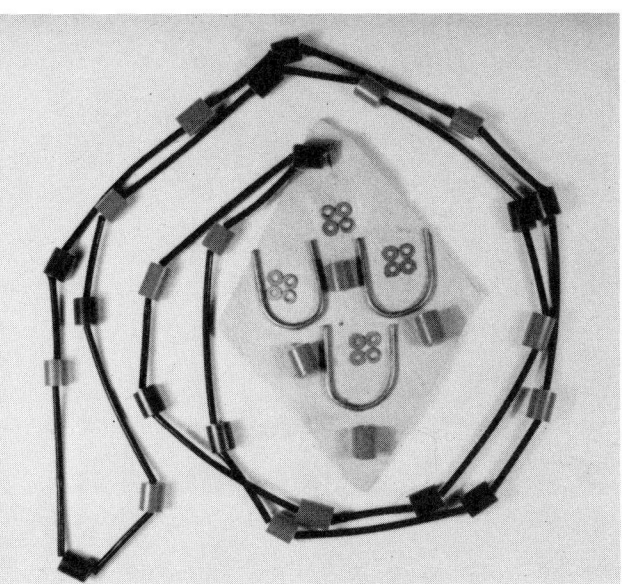

Fig. 2-3. Government surplus: leather and findings.

Three children's designs are shown in Figs. 2-2 through 2-4. The leather was cut with scissors and attractively combined with other materials by stitching, gluing and wiring.

Fig. 2-4. Suede and burlap.

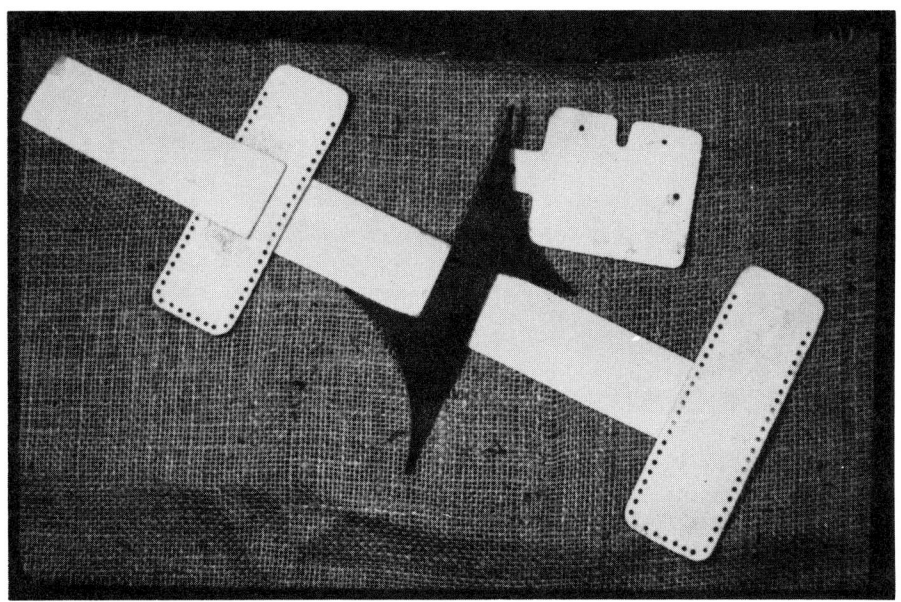

Fig. 2-5. Leather from an old vest.

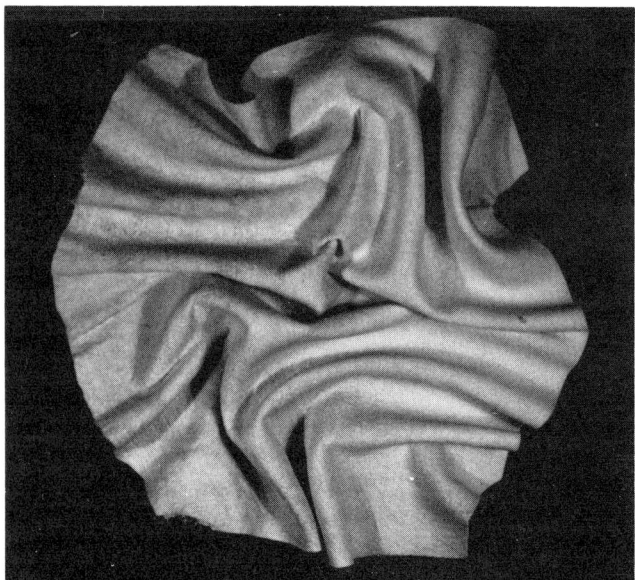

Fig. 2-6. Molded leather.

Hand crafted leather articles are treasured. They are beautiful; they feel good; they might even smell good. As with any craft, one can build a collection of special tools as skills develop. But a beginner working with salvaged leather can get along surprisingly well with a few common everyday tools, plus improvisation. Thick leather is too heavy to be cut with scissors. A steel straightedge guide should be placed along each line as it is cut with a utility knife. Tin snips are used to round corners.

In Fig. 2-5 a design was painted on the leather. Acrylic paints were used because of their flexibility. In addition to hand painting on leather, stencilling and printmaking can be done with acrylics, oil paints, oil printmaking inks or decorative paints made for use with leather surfaces. Richly stained, clean leather kept in good condition will always have universal appeal. A sensitive use of paints can heighten its appearance; if overdone, it can turn into a disaster.

Leather can be molded; molding is easiest with pliable leather. When leather is sufficiently dampened, it can be molded with hands or placed over a form. Upon drying, the leather will retain its new shape. Probably the best way to dampen a piece of leather is by sponging water on the back. When it begins to seep through the leather, darkening areas on the front side of the piece, sponge water on the front until it is absorbed evenly. The leather must not be overly wet, just damp enough for molding.

Fig. 2-7. Pyrography on discarded portfolio leather.

A design on paper can be transferred to dampened leather by placing the paper on the right side of the leather, holding the design in place with tape or paper clips. An outline of the design is now impressed in the leather with a ballpoint pen that has lost its ink or with an orange stick. A relief effect is created by raising and lowering parts of the design; this is where improvisation comes in. As long as the leather is damp, spoon-like instruments can be alternately rubbed over areas on both sides of the leather to shape it. Do this on a surface that will permit the leather to stretch into shape; a soft magazine will do.

On leather that is too heavy to be dampened and molded, pyrography—the process of burning designs—is used. The leather must be dry. A wood burning tool or a fine soldering iron is used to burn designs into it. Pyrographic designs are generally linear.

Fig. 2-8. Textured leather from worn jacket.

Damp leather can be textured by placing it on a hard surface and pressing into it any object that would make an interesting textural pattern. Striking the object with a hammer is one way to make uniform imprints over the leather surface. Almost any small object will make a lasting impression. Designs filed into nail heads or sanded into wooden dowels have been commonly used to express the individuality of the maker. With a very fine brush the texturing can be painted or stained for accenting.

Fig. 2-10. Wood; rope; leather.

Fig. 2-9. Bone; sponge; leather.

Fig. 2-11. Stone; leather; wood.

Don't overlook leftover short pieces of leather thongs. In each of the accompanying photographs the touch of leather was a significant contribution.

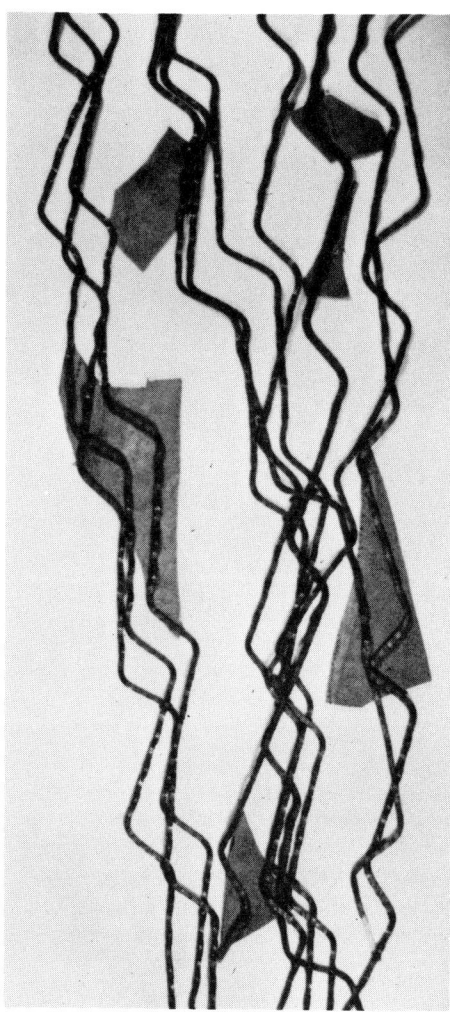

Fig. 2-12. Leather lacing and recycled car chamois.

Leather lacing can be braided, sprang and used in weaving and macrame.

When gluing lightweight leather to itself or other porous materials, as in collages, mosaics or appliqués, white glue is sufficient. Heavier leathers may need contact cement. Pieces of lightweight leather can be best sewn together by hand with a glover's needle and nylon, polyester or waxed linen threads. With machine stitching, use a long stitch and sew slowly. We have all seen pieces of leather laced together. Along the edges where the lacing is to take place holes are punched with a punching device, awl or ice pick. Decorative yarns, cords or leather thongs are laced through them with a tapestry needle in simple stitches or in a binding fashion. Skiving and beveling leather, setting grommets and designing with leather from animals such as reptile, seal and sheep hides are experiences that await those who learn through working with leather scraps and discovering how truly rewarding creating in leather can be.

Chapter **3**

OTHER MATERIALS FROM NATURE

Fig. 3-1. Felt tip pen on fungus.

Natural materials found in the woods, at the shore, under water, along the roadway or in the garden are being recycled into art forms.

Fig. 3-2. Sawed, sanded and stained pine; glued shells; shellacked.

Fig. 3-3. Silicone background; fabric dyed sand; mounted on plywood.

Sand, soil, gravel, crushed gem and rock can be used to make paintings or designs of naturally beautiful subtle hues. If necessary, experiment with dyes to change or darken the colors. Some of these natural materials may resist dyes. Sketch your picture or design on a rigid background such as cardboard, wood, Masonite, sand and gravel. Work on a flat surface. Brush on transparent drying glue where you want your darkest color to be and cover it with your painting material. Press down to aid the adhesion. Let dry, then quickly turn it upside down over a newspaper to catch the excess granules that did not stick to the glue. Lightly tap to be sure all loose particles are removed. If a heavier coating is desired, a second application is made. Continue in the same way with the rest of the colors. Rather than working from dark to light values, one could adhere the granular materials at one edge and work toward the opposite edge of a composition. If there is great variation in the structure of the materials used, the order of gluing is generally from fine to coarse. To crush rock: place it in a canvas bag on a hard surface and strike with a hammer until it is crushed. A mortar and pestle can be used to pulverize it further. Surprisingly, many rocks are not difficult to break.

Fig. 3-4. Dried wheat, pods, cockle burrs; feathers; shells; on weathered wood.

Fig. 3-6. Dried weeds; shells; rope; felt; tempera on heavy cardboard.

Fig. 3-5. Dried weeds with sawed, sanded and stained wood.

If you are using flowers, grasses, weeds or pods, pick them on a clear, warm or hot day from late morning until mid-afternoon. Flowers should be at the height of their bloom. There are several ways to preserve them. Hang them upside down for at least a week in a warm, dry place to thoroughly dry. Flowers and weeds without thick sections, such as violets, can be pressed between absorbent papers with a weight on top. The papers must be changed frequently. In dry weather allow a minimum of two weeks before removing the pressure and exposing them completely to the air. Faded colors can sometimes be restored by lightly applying water colors mixed with a detergent or thinned acrylic paints. Dyeing larger flowers is done, but all too often the colors are harsh and unnatural. Dehydrating formulas abound using such materials as sand, borax, sawdust, baby powder, alum and glycerine, but the chemical desiccant—silica gel —is popularly used to preserve fresh flowers. They are covered with this re-usable and granular composition for a few days.

There is yet another way designed to capture nature; by brushing on a tinted ceramic-like finish which requires no firing. Instructions for using commercial preparations come with the products. Whether you choose air-drying, pressing, desiccants or coatings, it is only through experimenting that familiarity is gained.

Fig. 3-7. Feathers; beads; leather.

With an accent on naturalism, feathers are used for jewelry. Notice the three personal expressions featuring feathers in Figs. 3-7 through 3-9.

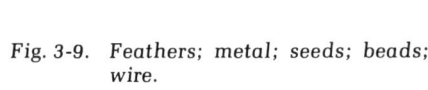

Fig. 3-9. Feathers; metal; seeds; beads; wire.

Fig. 3-8. Feathers; Brazil nuts; leather; wooden beads.

Fig. 3-10. *Feathers; bones; buttons; wood; glued to cork.*

Feathers combine well with many materials in wall plaques, pictures, weavings, collages and other art forms.

Fig. 3-11. *Feathers; shells; bones; buttons; yarn; fabric; sliced cork; glued to cardboard.*

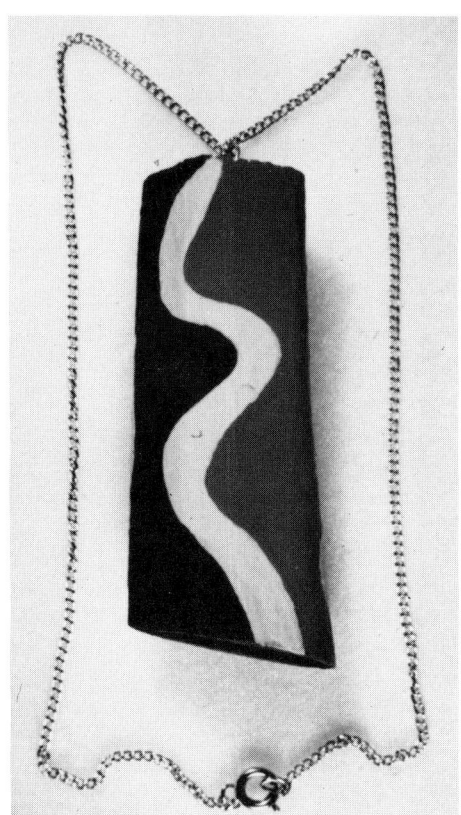

Fig. 3-12. Acrylic painted pendant.

Fig. 3-13. Stained bone; tree bark; dyed rice; glued to wood.

Fig. 3-14. Wishbone; wooden and plastic beads.

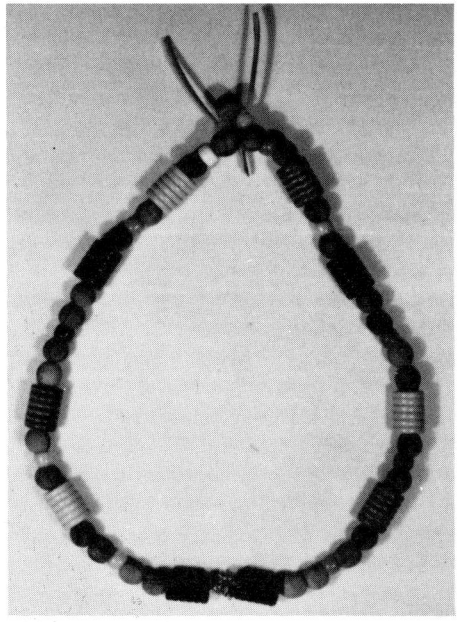

Feathers can be dyed by using food coloring, colored inks and fabric dyes. When gluing feathers, apply glue with a toothpick to the ribs or quills only. Gluing on the feathery parts matte down produces disappointing results.

From wishbones to soup bones, all kinds of bones are being recycled. Bones must be washed and bleached to lighten and clean them. Paint, stain, dye or leave them in their natural state. Bones may be carved, sawed or drilled. Scrimshaw, the art of carving whale's teeth, is limited because whale's teeth are not often available. Many carvers substitute large bones.

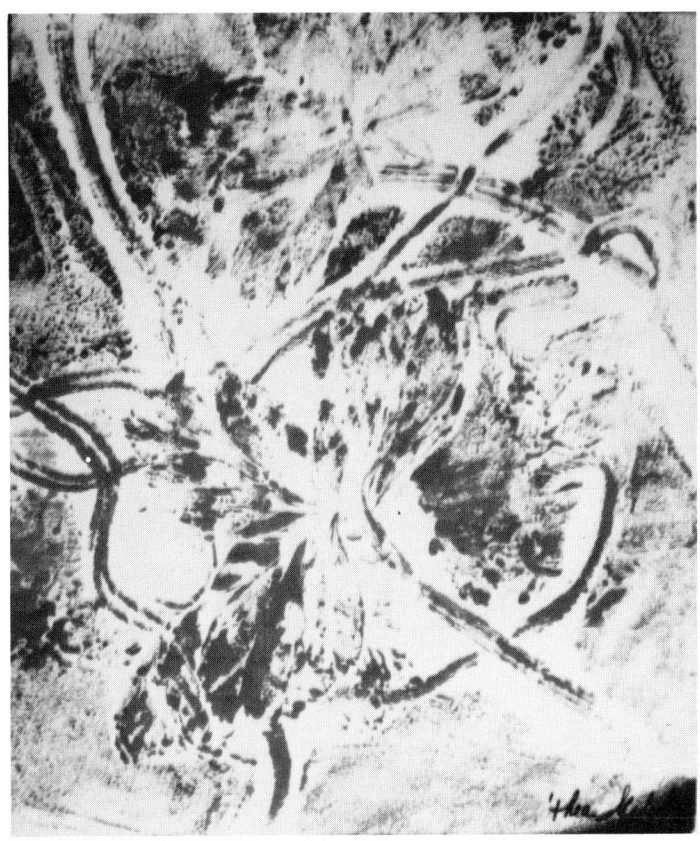

Fig. 3-15. Pachysandra print.

Nature serves us well. We are all familiar with the many uses made of pine cones, walnut shells, cornshucks and egg shells. Hobbyists, too, use nature's products as in carving peach pits and making apple head figures. Printmaking from nature is a quick process. For example, a brayer is evenly coated with block printing ink, then rolled over a leaf to color it. The leaf is placed with its inked side up on a clean surface. It is covered with a sheet of paper. Then gently rub over the paper with your fingers to make a leaf print on it.

Chapter 4
GLASS

One doesn't have to go too far afield in search of glass. Our personal possessions reveal glass in some form and every home continually finds ways to reuse it. Screw top jars are for storing things. Cheese and jelly jars turn into drinking glasses. Ketchup bottles remain in use as handy sprinklers. Burned out light bulbs make excellent puppet heads and maracas when covered with papier mâché.

Simply because parting with a handsome empty bottle can be a most difficult thing to do, it ends up with a lot of other good-looking bottles in the cellar or garage. There the collection waits for recycling. Outside the home, picture framing studios, auto glass specialists, glaziers, glass and mirror shops are sources for large pieces of scrap glass. When carrying large segments of scrap glass, protect the hands and tape the glass edges as soon as possible. For unusual finds and colored discarded glass, check glassware manufacturers as well as stained and leaded glass studios.

Fig. 4-1. Eyeglass-lens-and-feathers pin.

Glass has a slick, nonabsorbent surface making it difficult for many materials to adhere to it permanently. Be doubly sure that glass is absolutely clean before using. Even after washing with a detergent, check for streaking. Turpentine, rubbing alcohol or water and vinegar rubbed over the surface and dried with a lint-free cloth or paper towel aid in removing oil film and cutting grease. Do not handle the glass excessively. We tend to overlook the natural oils in our hands which render the glass even more resistant. The transparency of glass makes it possible to follow a design placed underneath it. Designing directly on the glass can be done with china marking or grease pencils. Some paints might resist them. This, of course, can be an advantage as well as a disadvantage. Graphite carbon paper can be used, but it erases easily. Lines can be drawn with permanent felt tip pens; rubbing alcohol removes them. Permanent felt tip lines might be incorporated into the final effect or covered with opaque paints.

Fig. 4-2. Discarded pane; glass stain (water based); acrylic; aluminum foil.

Fig. 4-3. Detail: room decoration crystalline effect.

Colorful transparent lacquers, cold process enamels, glass stains and permanent felt tip markers transparently stain glass. In addition to brushing, sponging and spraying, the liquid may be poured, quickly swirled around and drained out if the glass surface is concave. Used with restraint, crinkled aluminum foil behind a transparent glass design adds sparkle. Matte opaque paint in the areas around the design provides contrast and calls attention to the colorful scintillating design. Unless you use non-toxic products, be sure there is adequate ventilation when staining glass. An interesting effect is achieved with crystalline paints that resemble frosted window panes in winter. They come in a variety of colors and are easily washed off with warm water and soap or vinegar.

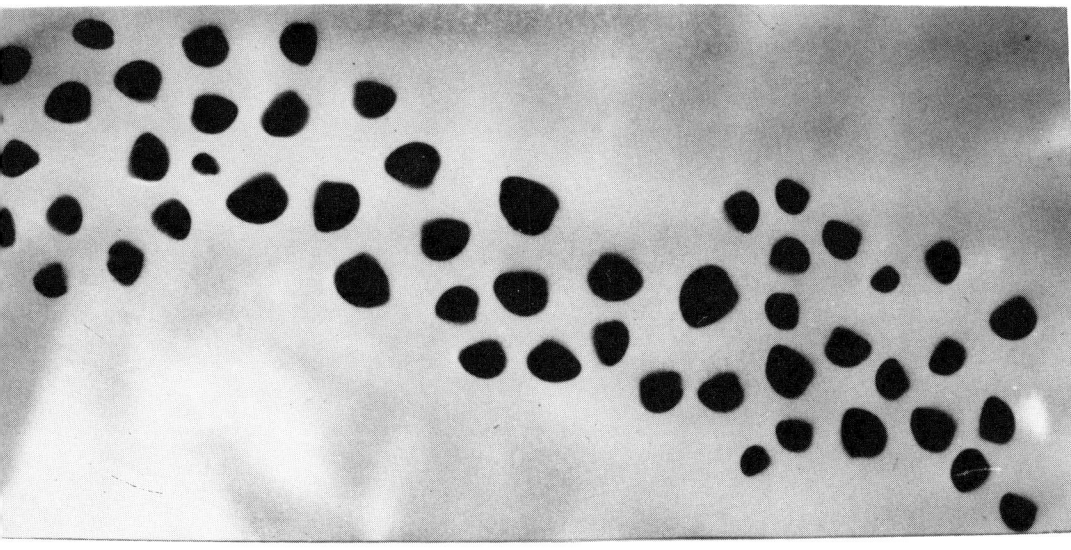

Fig. 4-4. Tinted frost design on salvaged glass.

Another way to change the appearance of transparent glass is to delicately frost a translucent design on the surface with commercial preparations that are easy to use. These products give the glass a little "tooth" to which paint adheres, if painting is necessary.

Fig. 4-5. *Gesso; tempera; matte medium.*

If your glass art will not receive too much handling, frequent washings or exposure to weathering, then oil paints with a slightly heavy consistency can be applied directly. It is disappointing to have paint pull away from glass or begin flaking after the work is completed. Paints adhere best to an impervious surface like glass if the surface is given a slight "tooth" by sanding or is covered with a base coat of gesso. How many coats of gesso to use depends largely upon the finish sought. One coat of gesso may suffice; two applied in opposite directions are better. Light sanding makes them smooth if this is important to the end result. Several white or tinted coats with clear acrylic sprayed between them (each layer allowed to thoroughly dry) can build into a marvelously opaque finish. The last few coatings may be gently sanded with soap suds and very, very fine sandpaper or emery cloth for an unusually smooth and rich looking surface. Most paints react favorably to a gesso ground. Spraying or brushing clear acrylic gloss or matte medium, varnish, shellac or nail polish over the paint is a protective measure. Take care in spraying not to disturb the paint; it may begin to bleed or shift.

57

Fig. 4-6. Painted glass structure.

Some jars and bottles are beautifully formed. Using them in combination can create exciting structures. Fill with sand if weight is needed. Colored water or ink, stones, shells and other memorabilia can be shown to advantage if the glass remains transparent. Glue bottles together with epoxy. Stain, paint, frost; use any or all of these.

Fig. 4-7. Acrylics on plaster impregnated gauze.

The quality and color of the glass in attached bottles might differ so radically that covering them is the best way to achieve unity. Plaster impregnated gauze carefully wound around the form adds texture while preserving the gracefulness of the bottle arrangement. A coating of plaster of Paris over the plaster-impregnated gauze will give another kind of texture. Sanding can be done if a smooth finish is desired. Plaster is a "thirsty" material; to prevent paint absorption, apply gesso before painting.

Fig. 4-8. Assorted materials; polymer medium.

A simple and effective way to cover glass bottles, jars and containers is to glue on cord, twine, sisal, rya, cotton rug yarns, braid or lightweight clothesline with color and pattern in mind. Paper, fabric or fur can be used, too. If you have permanence in mind when covering glass, be sure that the glue you use is made for a nonporous surface. Protective coatings of polymer medium, shellac or varnish prolong usefulness.

Fig. 4-9. Goblet and scrap glass.

Suppose the glass you find is not the size you want. It can be cut if it is not too thick. Using light and constant pressure, etch into the glass a continuous fine hairline from one edge of the glass to another edge with a glass cutter. Once is enough; do not go over the line. This is called scoring or scribing. Gently tap under the line along its full length to fracture or crack the glass. The opposite end of the cutter can be used; some have a little ball for this purpose. If you're quick, you can see the scored line widen in fracturing. This is generally sufficient to separate the glass; however, some cuts offer more resistance. Hold the glass in both hands—scored side up—and bend down lightly, or hold one end of the glass with taped flat pliers and apply gentle downward pressure. If this fails, there are two other ways. Heat the scored line over a candle flame. While the line is still hot, rub an ice cube over it. Heating then cooling the scribed line can be done by running hot then cold water over it as well. Nibbling is removing the small glass segments along the scored line which result when glass does not fracture with a clean cut. To do this, use the notches on the glass cutter or snap them off with taped pliers. If needed, glass can be sanded with sandpaper or emery cloth to smoothen the edges. Sometimes rubbing two pieces of glass together is effective. Glass must be scored from edge to edge one line at a time. That is why glass shapes are cut in steps. Placing a sketch of the shape under the glass enables you to figure out the lowest number of steps needed using straight and slightly curved lines. The edge of masking tape can be used as a guide for the glass cutter as it is pulled toward you until you develop confidence.

Glass cutting can be done quickly and is not difficult, but practice is necessary in developing the skill. It is wise to use safety goggles and protective gloves. Care must be taken, especially with extremely small glass fragments. Most bottle cutting devices evenly slice round bottles; they are not generally used for freehand cuts. In Fig. 4-9 we see an old glass goblet covered with assorted scrap glass cut into abstract shapes. They are mounted in grout grayed for contrast with waterproof India ink.

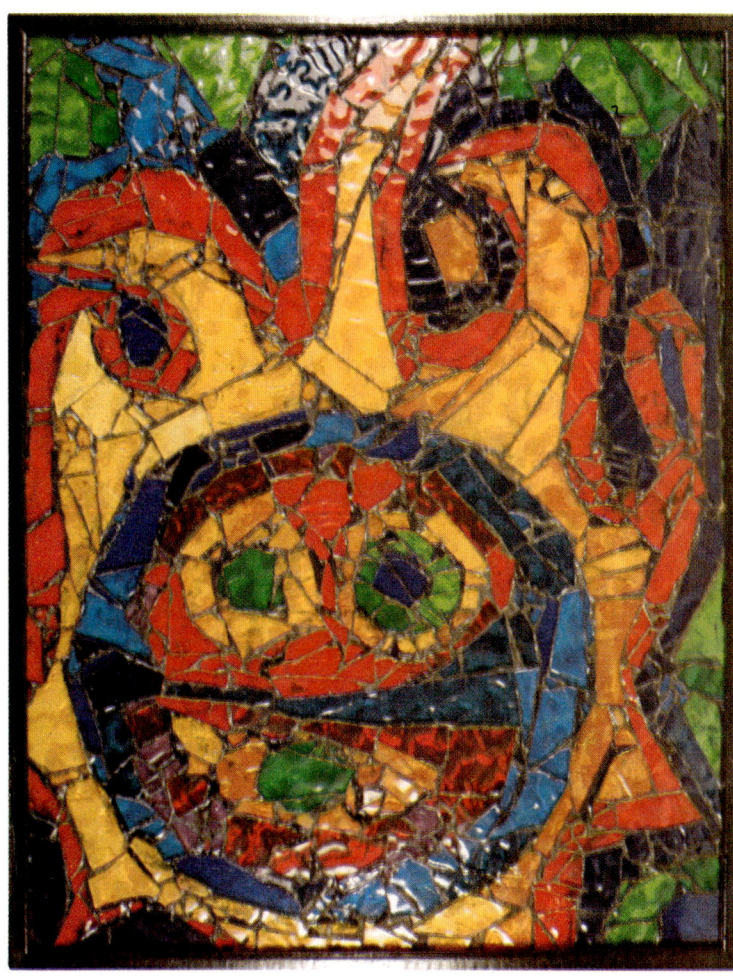

Fig. 4-10. Cut stained glass on wood.

If you are fortunate enough to have a number of glass pieces, they could be used to make a wall plaque, window, surface covering, or sculpture in a way that only you could think of. Spread the glass pieces before you. Select those shapes that have eye appeal. If some must be re-shaped or new pieces added, cut them with a glass cutter. What about their colors? If they are clear you might stain them or change their present colors by staining right over them. By mixing and blending stains you can get the exact jewel tones you want. Maybe you prefer opaque paints. Having some pieces opaque and some transparent might suit you better. Instead of having all the pieces plain some of them might have designs on their surfaces. The composition might be improved by overlapping or layering pieces. But however or whatever you do with them, there is always the question: How do I put them together?

In the goblet each piece of colored glass was placed against the clear glass of the goblet to permit light to pass through it, causing the color to scintillate in brilliance, especially in strong sunlight. The pieces were held in place by grout placed only between them. White translucent glass or plastic as a base soften brilliant colors placed against them. A solid background, such as plywood, does not permit light penetration and the effect is entirely different. The pieces may then be set directly in white or tinted grout to increase light reflection. The glass pieces are illuminated only by the light in front of them, since no light can enter from behind them.

Glass does not need any backing if the glass pieces are joined together with soft lead caming which encases the glass edges. In addition to glass pieces, one needs very soft U-shaped lead caming to wrap around the outer edges of the glass pieces located in the borders of the total design; very soft H-shaped lead caming for joining inner pieces together (one fitted into each side of the H); a utility knife for cutting the lead caming; steel wool to clean it; acid or rosin core solder; and a soldering iron—one that operates on 25 or 30 watts will do. The use of flux is optional. Solder can build up on the tip of the soldering iron; sponge it off frequently. Caming comes in long strips. To make this pliable lead hug the contours of the glass edges better, stretch it by stepping on one end while pulling the other end upward. Snugly bind each glass piece with the caming. Use the U or H shape depending on where the piece is located in the design and how it is to be joined. With planning, the number of soldered joints can be minimized. Touch the hot soldering iron to the solder; quickly rub it over the spot where the caming meets itself. This seals the lead edges together. Neatly solder the lead bound pieces together in the same manner. Beginners might get a solder lump or two which just won't melt away with the heat of the soldering iron. If they are objectionable, they can be filed away.

There is an alternate method. You need the same materials except that an adhesive backed copper foil, which comes in different widths, is used instead of lead caming. You could, of course, use both in your design. The copper foil is cut with scissors and bound around each piece of glass with your fingers. Should the tape need a little extra pressure in some spots to flatten it against the glass, gently use pliers with taped jaws to prevent the glass from getting scratched. The edges of the copper tape are soldered together where they meet; then the copper is completely covered with solder for added strength. This is called tinning. However, the copper tape adds a beautifully delicate effect and it does not have to be completely hidden with the solder. The encased pieces, tinned or not, are joined together with a drop or two of hot solder spread along adjacent edges. Fine copper wire can be soldered as part of the design or for support. The soldering looks very good, but the joints are not as strong as when lead caming is used. The copper foil method is best for small designs where there is less danger of the art form falling apart. Children can and do solder. This method is excellent to use for their first ventures in glass design.

Finishing the metal parts of the design depends upon your taste. Metals normally darken with time,

Fig. 4-11. Leaded stained glass.

Fig. 4-12. Leaded effect on discarded glass.

but this can be prevented. Solder, tinned copper and copper will remain bright if they are washed and dried, then covered with clear acrylic or lacquer. Lead caming is made brighter, and solder, tinned copper and copper are dulled by rubbing with fine steel wool. Wash, dry and coat with clear acrylic or lacquer. If an aged look is preferred, rub fine steel wool over solder, tinned copper or lead caming and cover with a copper sulphate solution. When dry, use clear acrylic or lacquer to cover the surface. Copper can be antiqued by brushing it with a solution of potassium sulphate, often sold as liver of sulphur. After it has dried, highlights can be made by lightly going over some of the surface with household cleanser on a wet cloth or fine steel wool. Protect the finish by sealing with clear acrylic or lacquer. If any of these surfaces are rubbed with sandpaper or steel wool, paint can be applied. A prime coat may be necessary to assure a bond between the metal and the paint. If you are thinking of using light-gauge copper sheeting and heavy copper wire in a design, a soldering iron that can reach a much higher degree of heat and a different type of solder are generally required. Experiment and see.

If you have salvaged a large piece of transparent or translucent glass, you can simulate the leaded glass effect without cutting glass or soldering. The simulation can be used on discarded glass objects, as well as on sheet glass, with equally good results. It works well on some plastic materials, too. The metal part of the glass design can be placed on a glass surface in either of two ways. You can use pliable one inch wide lead stripping which is sectioned into either eighths or quarters. They pull apart as needed. It comes in long lengths and can be cut with scissors. Adhesive is spread on the back of the strips when ready for use. When it dries, it will stick to the glass with slight pressure. Another method is to use a metallic compound which comes in a tube. Squeeze lead, steel, silver or gold directly where you want it to be on the glass and let it set. Whichever material you select, the simulation procedure is simple. Place your design under the glass or draw the lines on the glass with a permanent felt tip marker. Either place the adhesive coated tape over the lines or follow the lines in a continuous motion with the tube permitting the metal compound to flow evenly and smoothly. Stain or paint the areas within the metal lines.

Chapter 5
METAL, WIRE AND FOIL

To make major changes in scrap metal calls for tools which most people do not have. In recycling large or heavy pieces, only surface restoration is generally possible. It is not so important what the pieces were originally used for, as what the recyclist does with them. Reclaiming old pieces and seeing them in new relationships excites the imagination. Aging and weathering may have given the metal you find an appealing visual and tactile quality. If so, you're lucky; don't change it. Work with it. Most old metals, however, need to be cleaned. Wire brushing removes scales, but scratches the surface. Under opaque paint it might not matter. Sandpaper, turpentine, kerosene, mineral spirits, ammonia, steel wool, strong household cleaners and products specifically made for hard-to-clean metals all contribute to dirt, grease, grime and rust removal. Use what is available; it might clean the metal better than you think. Even if found metals are in good condition, surfaces must be free of grease and oil before using. Wash the surface with a detergent, rinse it with water and vinegar and dry it thoroughly.

If the art form is to be covered with opaque paints, first apply a sprayed or brushed metal primer as a rust preventative and sealer. Transparent stains, dyes

Fig. 5-1. Permanent felt tip markers.

and cold enamels can be used directly on bright, clean satin smooth metallic surfaces. Their luminosity is lessened if used over an opaque base coat. However, if the metal is not reflective, then a white or pastel opaque base is used. Spraying or brushing over stains and dyes with a transparent sealer such as acrylic polymer medium, varnish, shellac or lacquer retards metal corrosion. Sometimes, a few coats of a transparent sealer are used as a final finish regardless of whether opaque paints or transparent colors have been used. If the coats of sealer do not dry smoothly, each one is lightly sanded with very fine sandpaper or emery cloth. This can build into quite a handsome finish. Waxing and hand buffing add a final touch. Oxidizing which is a gradual darkening of exposed metal can be inhibited with a transparent sealer. Subjecting metal to intense heat will cover the surface with an array of iridescent colors that are preserved by covering the metal with clear varnish, shellac or metal lacquer.

Pliable aluminum from cans and food trays is readily cut with a scissor or metal snips. It can be easily embossed with a blunt object. Comparable light gauge copper has the same characteristics. With fingers, shaped pliers, slotted tools (a sardine can key

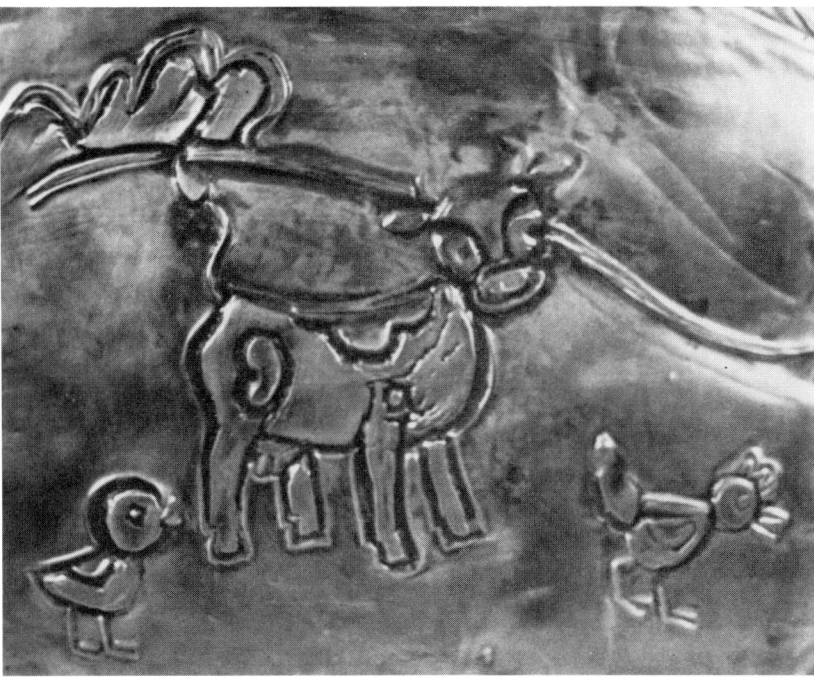

Fig. 5-2. Embossed metal can accented with permanent felt tip markers.

works well) or forming jigs, the flat flexible metal can turn into reliefs or three dimensional forms. Color is added with permanent felt tip markers, transparent glass stains, strong dyes or a thin application of glass-like cold enamel coatings. Heavy bodied opaque paints chip and crack on these flexible non-porous metals. Many things made in salvaged materials are not designed for posterity, such as decorations, party favors, scenery and play props. Through experimenting, ways can be found to make paint adhere even if only temporarily. Here are some suggestions: roughening the surface by sanding; applying a light coat of gesso; mixing tempera paint with detergent; using thin paint consistencies; spraying paint lightly; and adding to oil based paints a few drops of japan drier to hasten drying and improve the bond. With some designs, flexing of the metal can be controlled by attaching it to rigid cardboard. If the metal has more rigidity, using opaque paint is less of a problem. Metal primer as a base coat is recommended. Use one or two coats of primer, with or without sanding, and then spray or brush on paint. Those paints made especially for metal might suit your needs best. Of course, the transparent look can also be achieved as on the more flexible metals.

Fig. 5-3. Bottle tops and textured aluminum mounted on felt.

To prevent materials glued to metal from dropping off, use a flexible, clear-drying and waterproof bonding agent. Most glues or cements that are used with glass are used successfully on metal. They work equally well in joining and seaming metal to metal. With some thin pieces of metal staples can be used if they do not detract from the design.

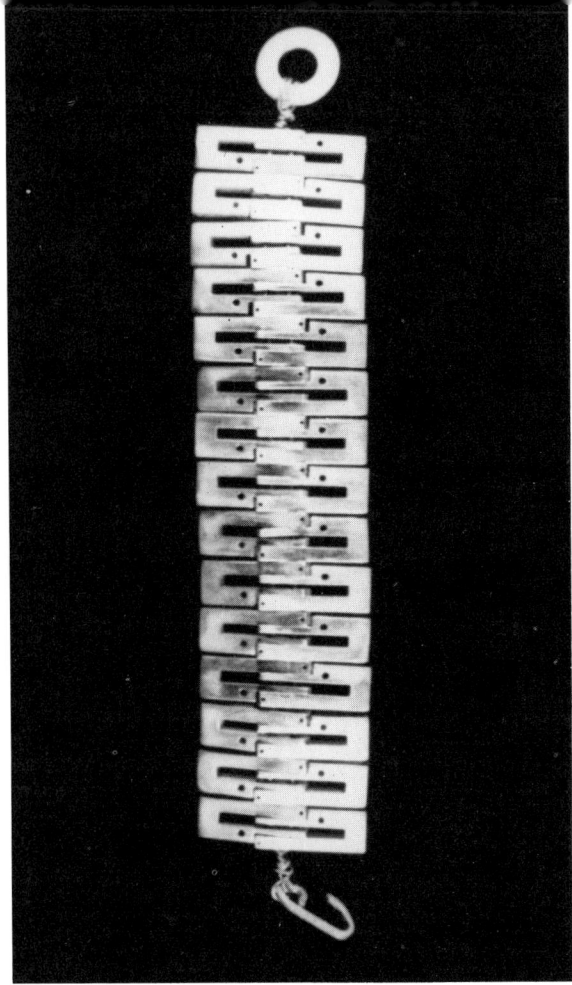

Fig. 5-4. Government surplus; pieces flexibly wired in series.

The design potential in salvaged metal parts is tremendous. There are four elegant pieces of jewelry in Figs. 5-4 through 5-7. In each one, the dominant piece of metal had a number of holes in it. Notice how differently it was attached in series, or to other pieces of metal, in each of the pictures.

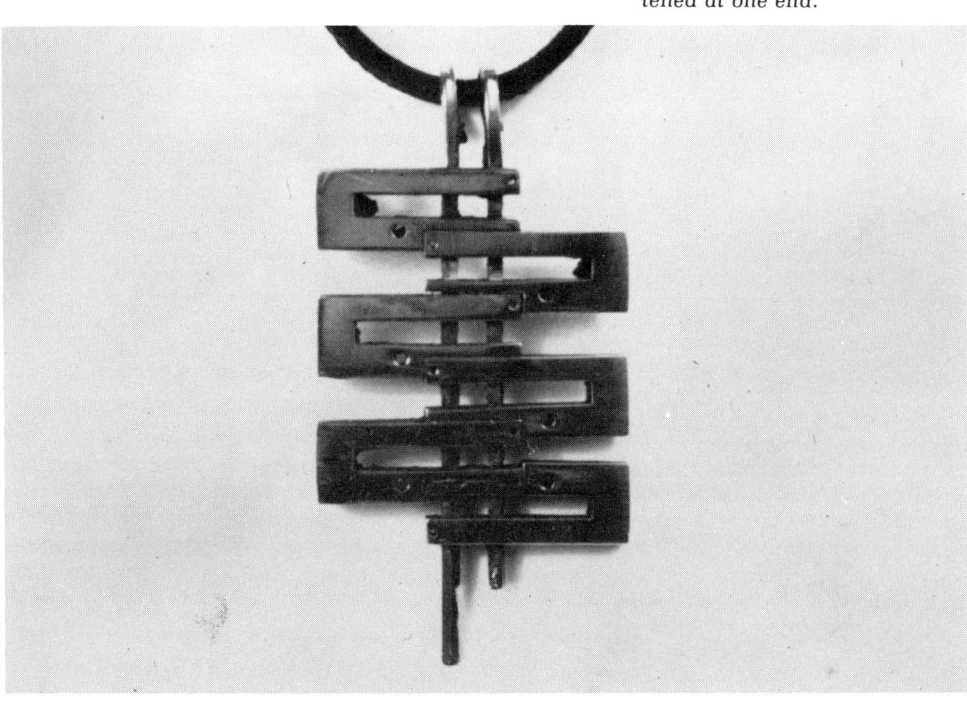

Fig. 5-5. Government surplus; pieces alternated on looped rods flattened at one end.

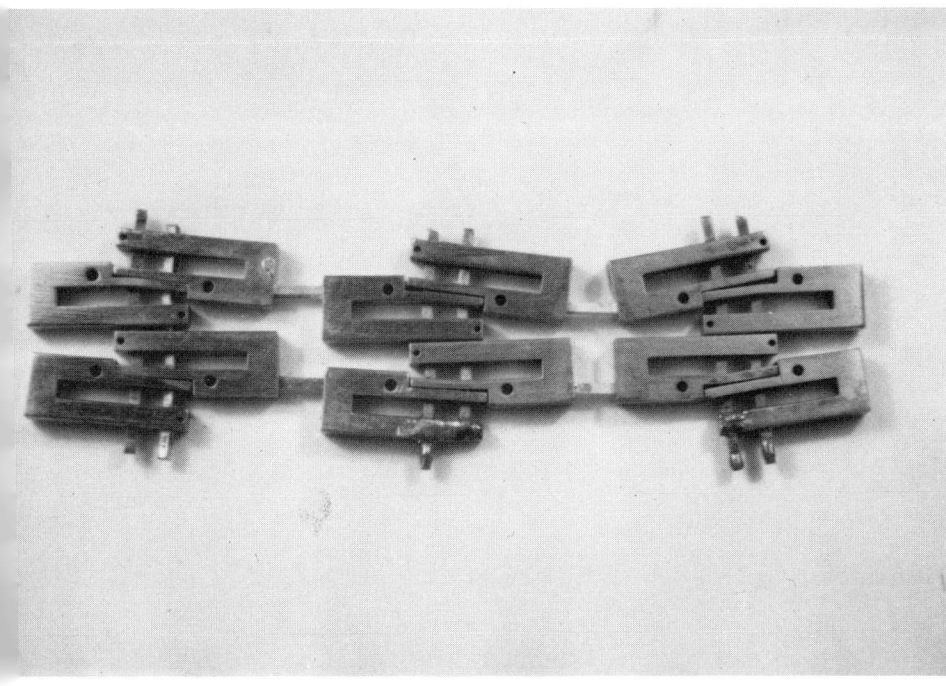

Fig. 5-6. Government surplus; pieces alternated on heavy wire flattened at ends.

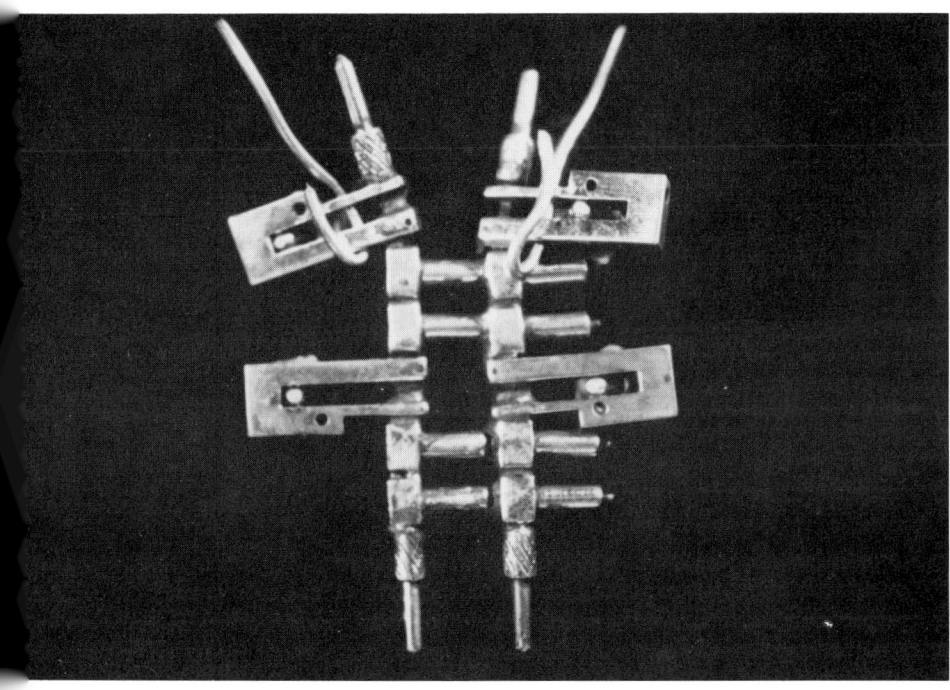

Fig. 5-7. Government surplus; pieces attached to mating parts.

Fig. 5-8. Cans covered with sateen ribbon and buttons; flexible joints.

Fig. 5-9. Can lid; wood; metal parts.

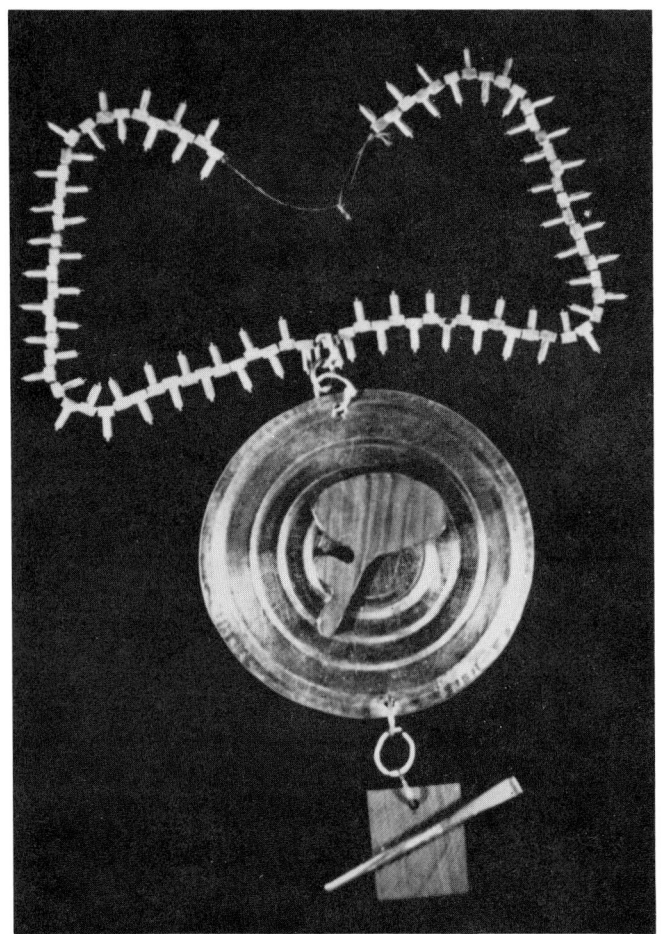

Holes may be needed to tie metal parts together. Punch holes in the metal with a hammer and a nail, or use a hand operated can opener (the kind that can puncture holes), an awl or an ice pick if the metal stock is no heavier than that of cans. Holes in thicker metal would have to be drilled. To tie cans together in series use a needle long enough to carry cord, or elastic cord for flexibility, through each can as it is joined to another. A needle can be made by snipping a light metal coat hanger into a convenient length and bending an eye at one end to hold the cord. There is a way of joining metal to metal which does not lend itself to permanence, but parts can be interchanged at will. Cut slits in each piece wide enough and deep enough to hold other pieces when they are slipped into the slots. Sculptures are easily built in this manner.

Cans in all sizes and shapes are being used in recycled art. If they are opened with can openers that eliminate rough edges, then the chances of cut fingers are lessened. Serrated shears eliminate sharp edges when cutting shapes out of a can. Strips can be curled with a slotted curling tool. It resembles a screw driver with a slit at the tip. For many years a myriad of uses have been found for cans after their contents are emptied; in the process, they have been covered, painted and camouflaged.

Fig. 5-10. Elevated bottle tops; small enameled dish; glued to felt.

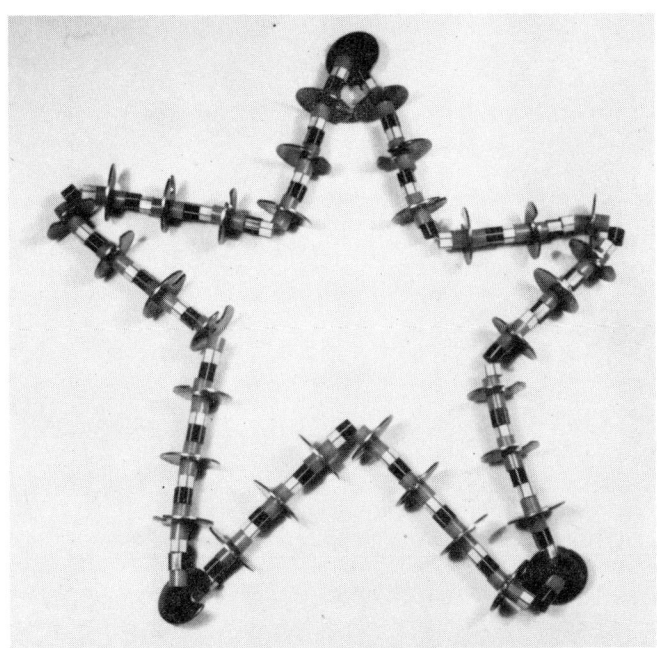

Fig. 5-11. Metal discs; plastic findings; strung on nylon fish line.

It is difficult to cut shapes by hand if a heavy-gauge metal is used. Draw the shape on the metal with a permanent felt tip marker. Shears made especially for use with metal will give you a rough cut. You will have to use a saw or file designed for use with metal to remove the excess material. If the piece is to be textured, place the metal shape on a resilient surface such as a bed of newspapers. Many metal shapes, for example large nail heads, can be used for texturing by striking them with a hammer on the surface to be textured. Using a ball-peen hammer directly on metal gives an attractive texture. A piece of metal might be enhanced by contouring it over a round or angular object and applying pressure with the hammer or fingers. A composition mallet will not mar the surface. Placing a block of wood over metal before striking with a hammer prevents hammer marks.

Lift-up can tabs, bottle tops and keys are a few of the many metal items we can gather. Machine shops are great sources for discarded metal, especially the shaped pieces from punch press operations.

Fig. 5-12. Chicken wire cage with found objects.

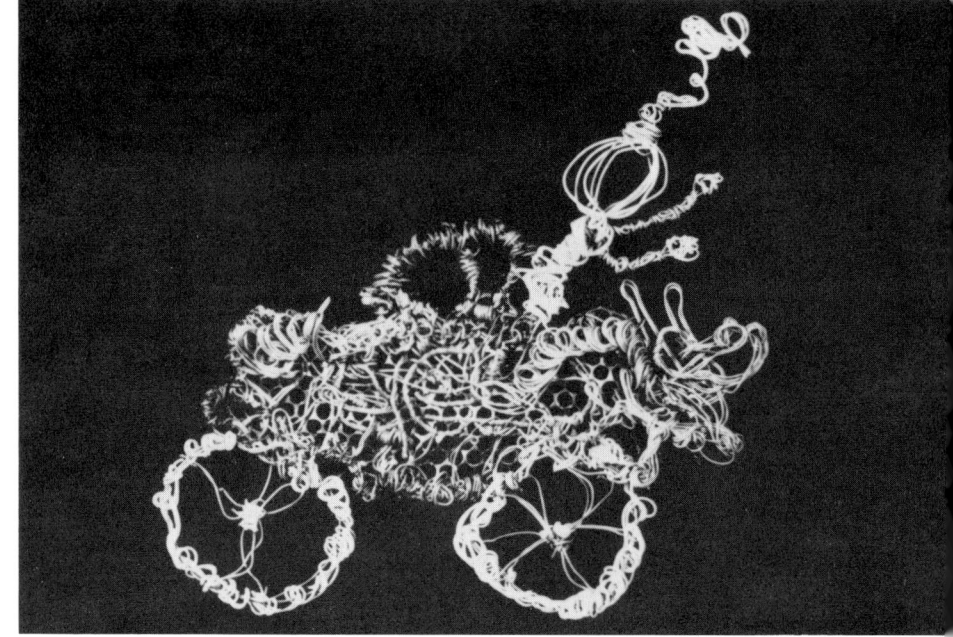

Fig. 5-13. Wound telephone wire and perforated plastic strips used in making sequins.

Leftover pieces of chicken wire, fencing and screening are not difficult to find. Wire can be salvaged from any firm dealing with electrical part, appliances or products. Manufacturers making wire forms have scrap wire or metal stripping. In addition,

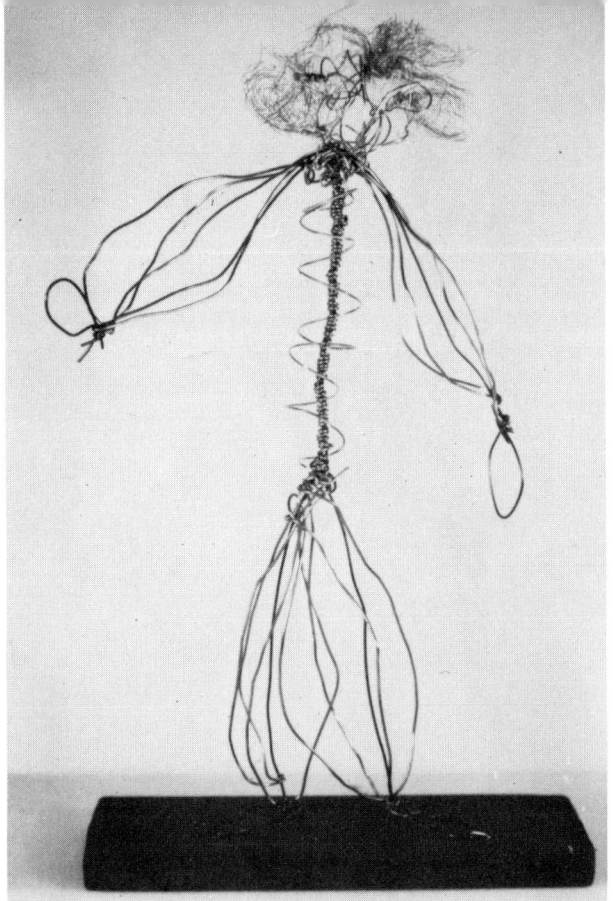

Fig. 5-14. Assorted wires on wood block.

Fig. 5-15. Coat hanger wire; paper; wire; painted clay apples.

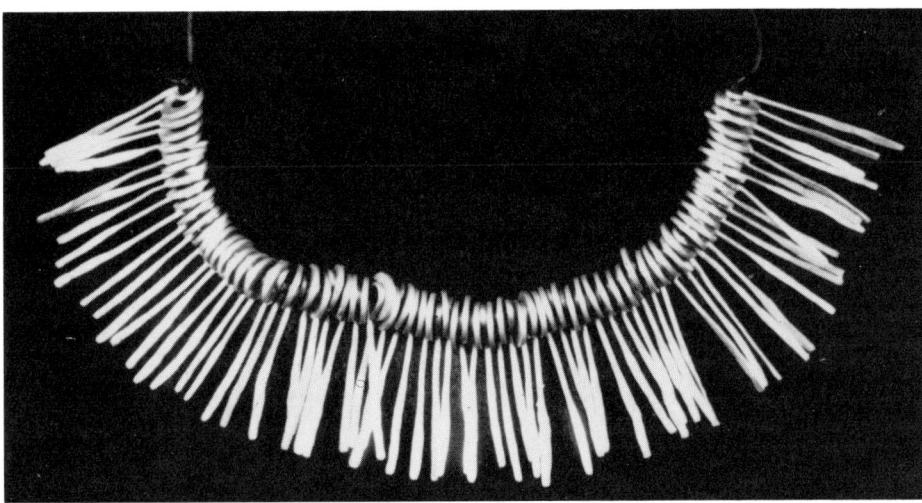

Fig. 5-16. Hammered and formed wire on leather.

many home workshops have scrap wire. Cleaning out the more than half used spools of wire; searching for the little piece here and the little piece there; getting out the metal snips and pliers (different noses add variety); all these initiate adventure with wire design.

Flattening some areas of a wire is most effective, but do not work the metal too much. The wire will begin to stiffen and can become brittle enough to break. Periodically annealing the wire by subjecting it to intense heat restores it to a workable state.

74

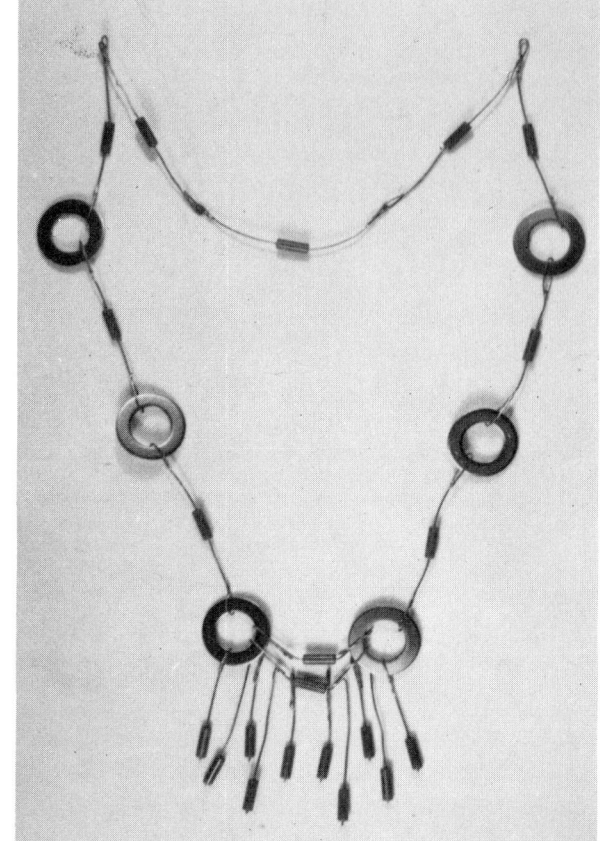

Fig. 5-17. Metal and plastic parts wired and soldered together.

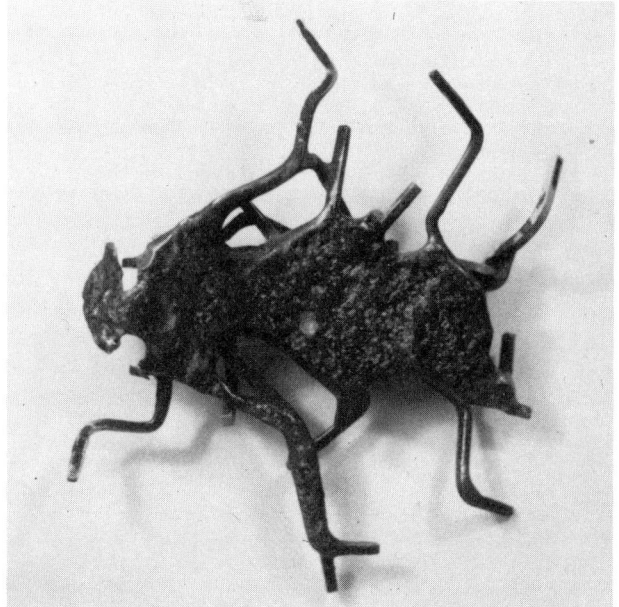

Fig. 5-18. Melted solder and wire bug.

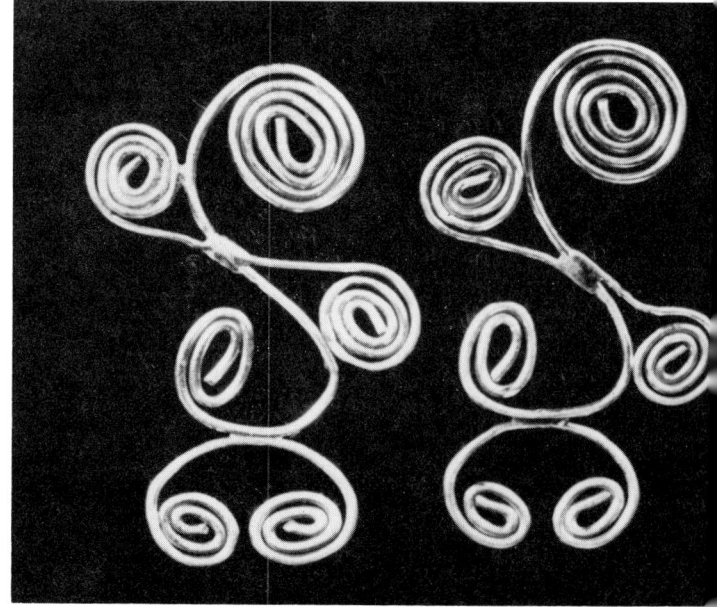

Fig. 5-19. Soldered coiled wires.

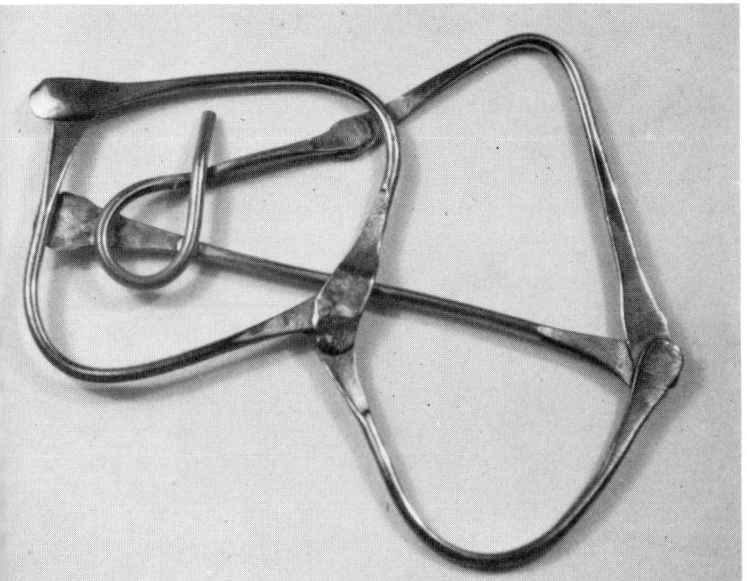

Fig. 5-20. Hammered and soldered wires.

Fig. 5-21. Soldered wires and metal.

Sometimes soft solder can be used to join two wires together. It is handy for applying jewelry findings such as ear clips and pin bars. Soft solder melts around 450°F and a low wattage soldering iron is adequate. Flux can be applied to the joint to be soldered to promote the fusion of the metals and control oxidation. The solder is placed over the area where the soldering is to take place and the tip of the soldering iron quickly applied to melt it into place. Binding wire is often used to hold the joint together while being soldered.

Fig. 5-22. Metal foil relief.

Metallic foils come in very light gauges and several hues. Some are self-adhering and others are paper-backed. The most common scrap available will be the light and heavy gauged aluminum foil usually found in the home. Although possessing about the same qualities as the pliable metals, foils tear easily and can be crumpled by hand. This is used to advantage in art and a number of uses are being found for the foils. Here is one. On a sturdy surface glue a relief design made with any materials, but avoid sharp edges which might pierce the foil. Cardboards, strings, cords, buttons, washers and sliced old crayons are examples of good materials to use. Crinkle the foil and straighten it out. Be sure that the foil is free from grease. Dilute clear drying glue with a little water. Spread it over the design. Place the foil on top. Gently press in and around the design. The foil must hug the entire relief. It can be colored with transparent materials such as permanent felt tip markers before crumpling. After the foil is glued in place it can be painted. A light brushing of paint fills the crevices leaving surface areas unpainted. Instead of paint, colored inks can be used. It may be necessary to mix a little detergent with them to make them adhere. Dark inks create an antique look. A sealer may be used for extra protection.

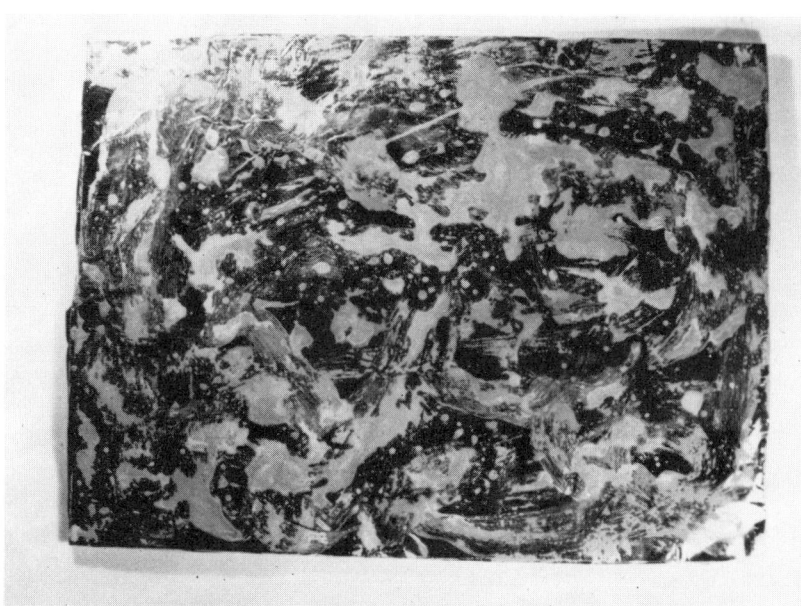

Fig. 5-23. Textured foil; dripped paint.

Chapter **6**

STRINGS AND FABRIC

Fig. 6-1. Cardboard disc; yarns and beads.

Creative expression using odd assortments of strings, threads, ropes, cords, yarns or other linear materials is limitless. Using them alone or in combination with other materials demands an imaginative approach, because it is most unlikely that a duplication of one is personal scrap collection exists elsewhere.

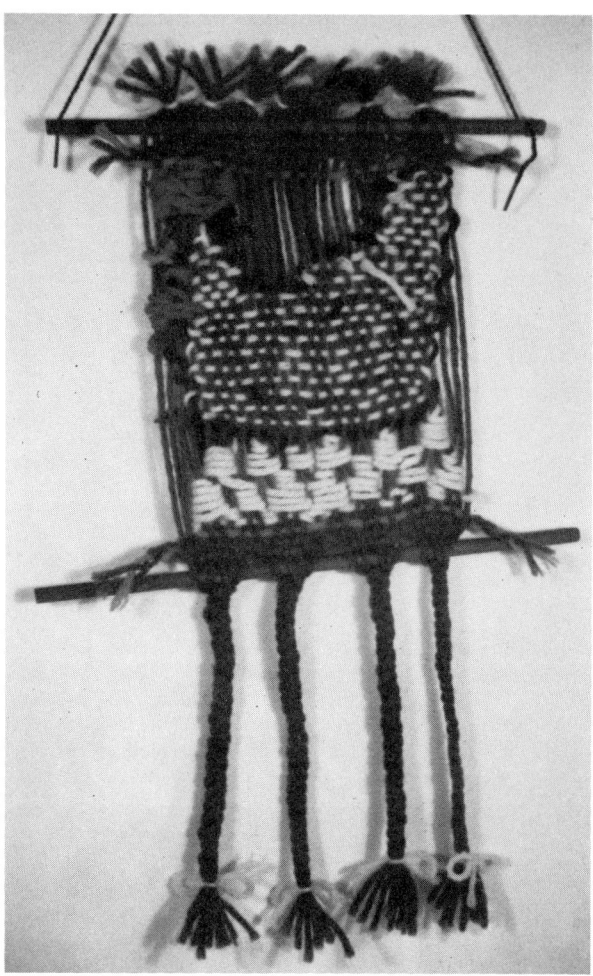

Fig. 6-2. Dowels; woven and plaited yarns.

Fig. 6-3. Group participation; woven faces.

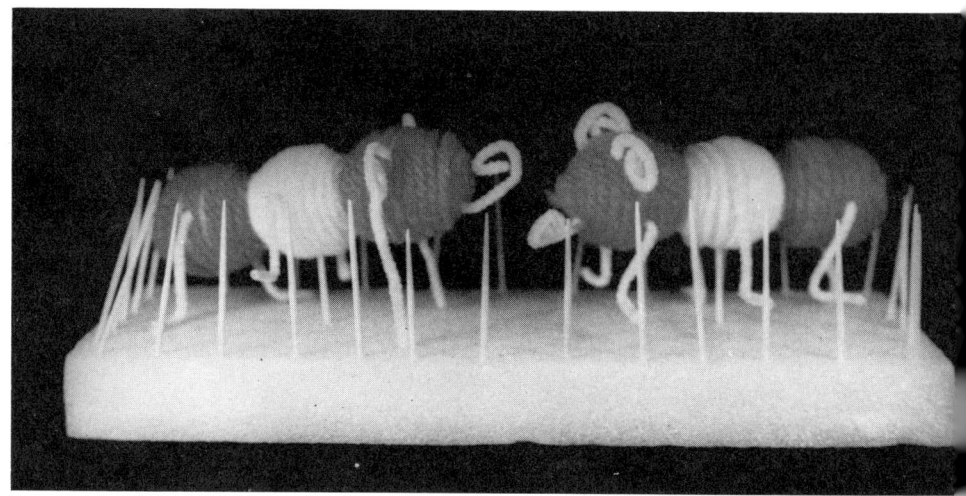

Fig. 6-4. Yarn; pipe cleaners; toothpicks; white plastic foam.

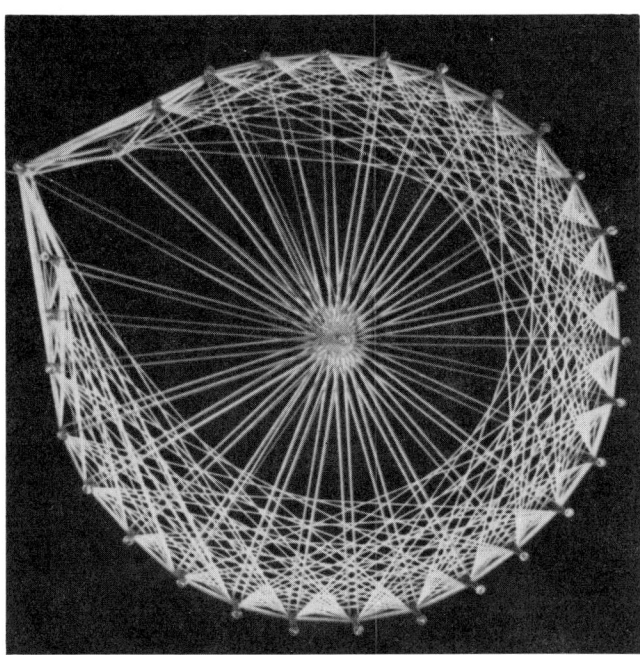

Fig. 6-5. Thread; brads; velvet on plywood.

Fig. 6-6. Strings; nails; stained and waxed wood.

Leftover strings, sewing and crochet threads, embroidery floss and cords can be put to good use in symmography—the art of string design—which lends itself to as much originality as anyone wishes to bestow upon it. At the same time string art can be tackled by a novice with little danger of the project's turning into a disaster. A piece of soft wood (or comparable material), nails and hammer, and you are ready to design with your strings. Is the wood interesting as it is: weathered, grained or unusually marked? Would a stain enhance it or is covering with paint or fabric needed? A design can be drawn directly on the wood or worked out on paper and transferred to the wood. An alternative way is to hammer in the nails then let a design unfold by itself as the strings are wound around them.

To eliminate nails projecting from the background holes can be made and string pulled through them with a crochet hook. The string can also be threaded through the holes with a tapestry needle. Since no nails are then required, cardboard can be used for the background.

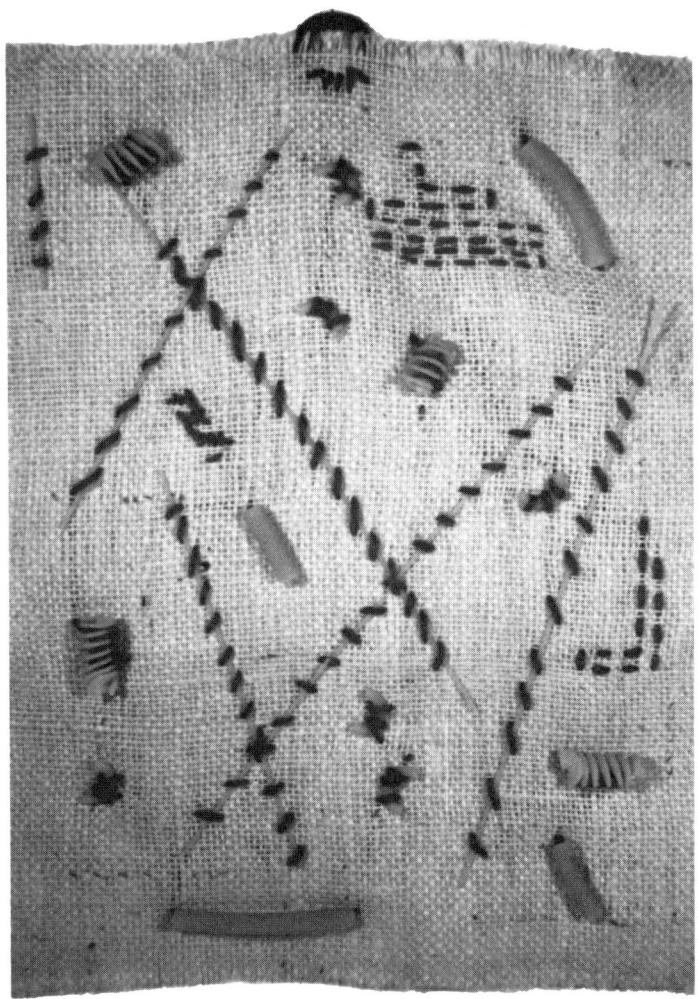

Fig. 6-7. Couching stitch over pasta.

Scrap yarns, strings, lightweight clothesline or cords are suitable for string drawings and designs. A line drawing is done directly on the fabric or transferred to the fabric with carbon and made permanent by stitching along the lines. Combining a variety of materials in making the lines adds color and textural interest. When using heavy cord or yarn, place it over the lines of a linear design and attach it by couching. Invisible couching is done with a fine thread to catch the heavy cord or yarn to the fabric from underneath. The couching stitch is visible when a finer thread from underneath is looped over the heavy one and becomes part of the design. Objects may be couched to fabric as well.

Fig. 6-8. Glued cord on burlap; felt accents.

The beautifully colored and honey combed pliable wax sheets (about 8" × 16") used for making rolled candles possess the natural stickiness of beeswax. The sheets are soft enough to be cut with scissors and small objects can be pressed into them or glued on. By applying gentle pressure with finger and orange stick, yarn can be made to stick to the slightly sticky wax surface. The yarn does not have to be deeply imbedded nor does the wax sheet have to be completely covered. Placing a cloth or newsprint over the wax sheet and quickly pressing a warm iron over it is sufficient to adhere the wax sheet to a support. Stapling, pinning and gluing are other ways to attach the wax sheet. A completed design can be sprayed for permanence.

As an alternative, use a transparent drying glue. By coiling the cord a solid shape is made. It is easier and sometimes neater to glue it together on waxed paper or household plastic wrap. When dry, the coiled shape is attached to the background of the design.

Fig. 6-9. Pearls, fine and heavy yarns in beeswax.

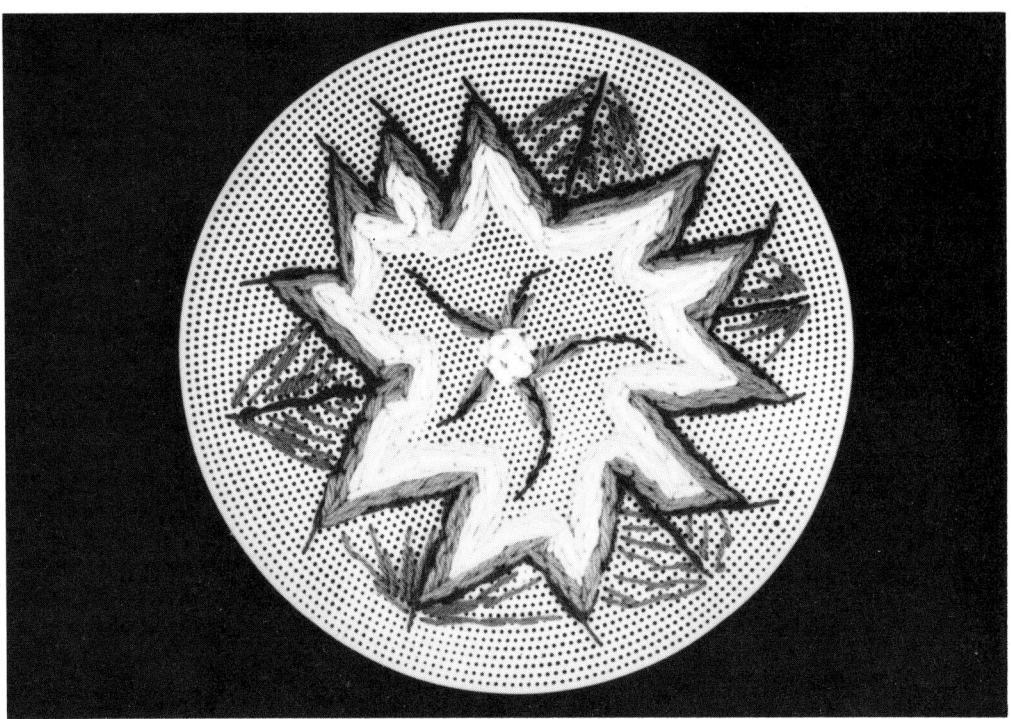

Fig. 6-10. Yarn on perforated plastic.

It was only a question of time before a lightweight, perforated and easily cut plastic would be available for weaving, bargello and needlepoint. It is ideal for using small leftover pieces of yarn, cord, sisal —anything that can go through the openings. The plastic stays true to the size and shape cut, even in miniscule. It eliminates the frustration often encountered in needlework, making it ideal for children to use. The plastic does not necessarily need framing and can be used for mobiles, wall hangings, jewelry and room dividers.

Fig. 6-11. A variety of yarns and stitches create the design—contoured with plastic bags.

If you have a variety of colorful yarns, strings or any other linear materials, but not quite enough of any one quality or color to make a completely satisfying design, then needle painting is the answer. It is at its very best when bits of this and bits of that are used. And the most fun, too! Look over your collection. Do more than that. Handle the yarns: slippery, rough, fuzzy textures; muted, crisp, shocking colors. Do they nudge old memories of things experienced; stir feelings through association; or excite you sufficiently to get started and see what happens? Whatever—the major step has been taken! Gather a few different sized needles, scissors, a background material and, perhaps, a supporting frame to keep the background rigid, making it easier to work on. The texture and color of the background fabric can be incorporated into the picture or design.

Yarn painting can be done without needles, too. Scraps are pasted to a background as described in string drawings and designs but emphasis is on shape rather than line. The background need not be fabric since needles are not involved in the process.

Fig. 6-12. Felt and cord on burlap.

If you add to your collection of linear materials, scraps of assorted fabrics, you can try your hand at sabrina. This was an English movement started about the middle of the last century and was soon occupying the time of many ladies even beyond the British Isles. It appears to have been named after a legendary princess of ancient Britain who was turned into a water nymph. The connection is not clear because its aim was to recycle into art any materials left over from garments sewn at home. Unless, of course, this fabulous princess of a remote age recycled, too! At any rate, the method, whether originating here or not, has persisted, appearing under different names around the world. Today in America, we refer to it as appliqué combined with creative stitchery. As in days past, the technique is applied by individuals uniquely reflecting the time and generation of which they are a part. Furniture stores, upholstery shops, remnant counters and economy shops are sources if you are short of materials. Never discount the many pounds of no longer needed fabrics such as sheeting, towels, blankets and clothing that consumers dispose of yearly. Sabrina is a design of fabric scraps outlined and complimented with attractive stitches on a suitable background. Do not despair if you have never done any creative stitchery. Diagrams and instructions are constantly available through magazines, pamphlets, books or sewing centers. If you know two stitches, that is enough to get started. Keep it simple. Omit the stitching if the invisible drying glues of today can do a satisfactory job for you.

Fig. 6-13. Sculptured fabric.

Padding or stuffing an appliqué design adds a sculptured look: puffy cheeks on a smiling child; billowing sails on a boat; and raised areas of an abstract design. We readily recognize this technique as the traditional and functional quilting or trapunto work with cotton batting as the stuffer. However, in some contemporary art almost anything becomes the filler and the long hours spent in stitching are eliminated. Suppose the appliqué were a fish shape cut out of material. Scale markings, gill and mouth are identified by yarn glued on the fish. The eye becomes a sequin. Plastic bagging, nylon or any material that would make a soft contour is glued on the reverse side in the areas to be padded. It doesn't take too much glue—just a drop or two. Padding is tapered to the outer edges. The fish shape is placed over the spot where it will be permanently glued to see how it looks. When the appearance is satisfactory dots of glue are applied over the underside of the fish and the edges lightly outlined with glue.

Sculpturing does not necessarily need a background. The same process is used, but instead of cutting out one fish, two could have been cut to make a three-dimensional form. Details would be glued on both of the pieces remembering that when they are joined there will be a front and back to the sculptured fish. Padding would be lightly glued between them and pressed into place. The outer edges could be taped, glued, stapled or sewn together. Several kinds of fish could be stuffed and layered into an arrangement making an interesting fabric sculpture. Variations abound because no rigid rules exist. Some marvelous results have been achieved by people wanting to express their ideas and going about it in their own way.

Fig. 6-14. Fabric; paper; water color felt tip pen.

All sorts of imaginative things are being done with fabric remnants.

Fig. 6-15. Some warp and weft burlap threads pulled; woven necklace and feathers; stitchery.

87

Fig. 6-16. Fabric; felt; yarn; cardboard.

Fig. 6-17. Felt shapes on cardboard.

Fig. 6-18. Felt; burlap; shagged cotton yarn.

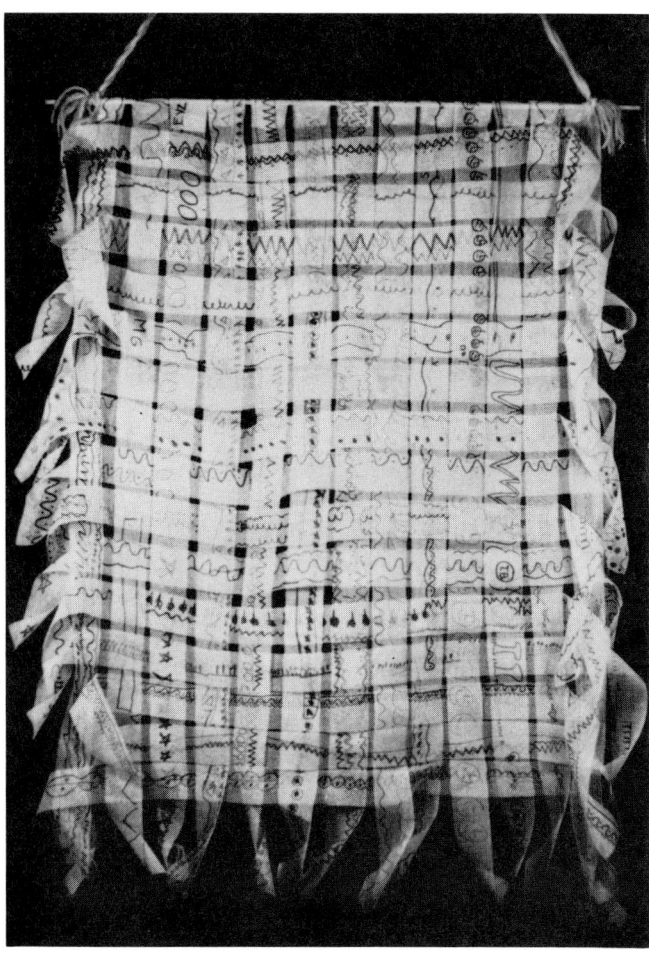

Fig. 6-19. *First grade class activity; woven organdy; permanent felt tip pens.*

Liquid crayons, felt tip pens and markers have rekindled interest in the age-old art of painting on fabric. They are quick, clean and easy to use. Water-based ones wash out; rubbing alcohol causes bleeding with most others. Centuries ago the Chinese painted on their beautiful silken fabrics and on tree pulp treated to resemble velvet. Much later in history, Europeans painted on velvet and it was much admired. By the end of the eighteenth century, theorem or stencil painting became popularized and reached America. It remained a genteel art, never taken too seriously, because less fragile backgrounds were more practical for painting. However, painting on fabric continued to be one of the minor arts useful for personal and home adornment. With strides made in modern painting and current interest in unique batik methods of dyeing fabrics, many people are experimenting with painting on fabrics. Paints and inks made expressly for textiles, acrylics, temperas, finger paints, oil paints, caseins, food colorings, dyes, colored inks and stains are being used. Fabric absorbs paint; through practice, one soon gets the "feel" of the proper paint consistency needed for different effects. When using oil based paints and inks, squeeze a small amount out of the tube onto a blotter. Allow the excess oil to be absorbed before using.

Fig. 6-20. Hand painted muslin sheeting.

Painting directly on linen is pleasurable. Closely woven and smoothly textured silk, wool and cotton generally take paint very well. Synthetics vary. A little practice in handling the paint on napped fabrics such as velvet, sleek surfaces such as satin, and matted materials such as felt is needed. Test fabric before using. Many are treated with repellent finishes which will not readily take all paints. When manufacturing fabrics, fillers are sometimes used. After washing, noticeable shrinkage often occurs and the fabric becomes limp. If your work must withstand launderings and you do not know the structure of the fabric, wash the fabric first. Creative stitchery is often used to accent hand painted fabrics.

Of all the processes ever devised for designing on fabric, batik holds the most fascination. Even the simplest design looks complex only because of the way wax is used to repel dyes. The origin of batik is lost in antiquity; Europeans were introduced to it through Dutch merchants returning from Malaya and Java with native fabrics. The principle of batik, as used today, is simple. Hot wax is applied to areas of the fabric which are not to be dyed. The lightest colored dye is applied first, either by painting on the fabric or by dipping the fabric into the dye. In either case, the wax resists the dye and what is hidden under the wax is not affected by it. The fabric is then rinsed and dried. It is placed between sheets of newsprint or wrapping paper and a warm iron is rubbed over the papers to melt the wax in the fabric. When the wax is removed, the process can be repeated by blocking out other areas with hot wax and using different colored dyes until the design is completed. The marbleized effect, so characteristic of batik, is done by gently crushing the waxed areas or by scratching them with a pin, needle or toothpick before using a dye. This allows small trickles of dye to form web-like patterns.

While admiring the batik effect, many have shied away from doing it either because it uses hot wax or because batik can be a lengthy process. Both objections have been overcome. There are cold water waxes that can be washed out of fabric with warm water and a detergent. The crackle effect is less pronounced. Regular household waxes are used with varying degrees of success, because removing them from material is not easy. With the hazards of working with hot wax eliminated, batik is brought within the reach of very young children.

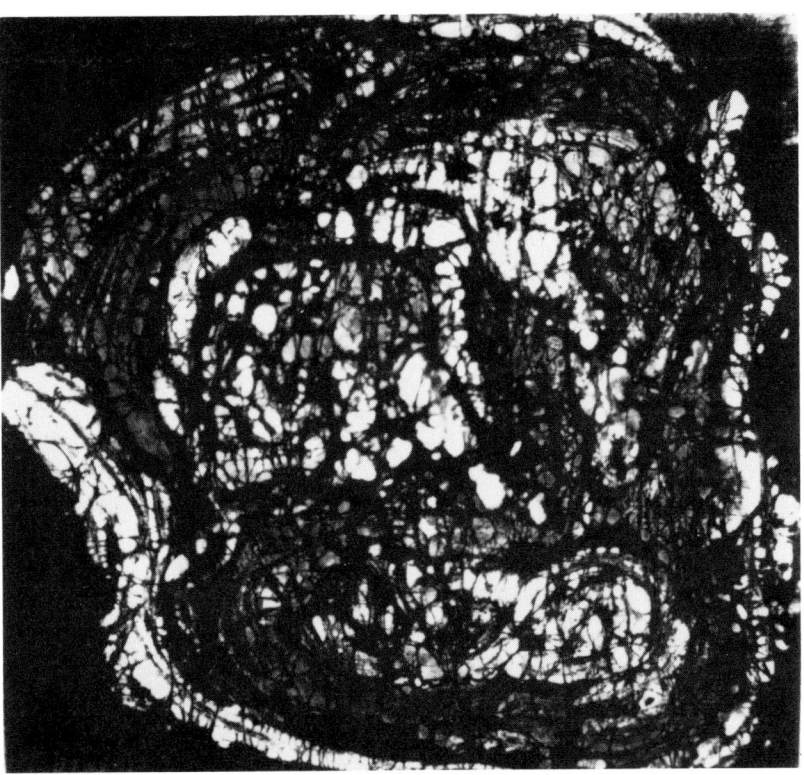

Fig. 6-21. Crayon batik on light drapery remnant.

Either a commercial product which combines wax and color or colored crayons and paraffin wax shorten the batik process. When melted with crayons, paraffin makes a mixture that permeates fabric more easily. It also gives a more pronounced batik crackle effect if the fabric is crushed before dyeing. One has to judge the amount of paraffin to use. Colors are individually melted in small tins placed in larger pans filled with water over low heat. The molten wax is brushed on the fabric with natural bristle brushes. A traditional tjanting needle may be used to trail fine wax lines, but it is not absolutely necessary. The fabric is tacked to a frame or placed over waxed paper. A design may be drawn on it with pencil or directly with the hot wax. Since the colors are in the wax, the entire design is waxed in one step with no particular color sequence. The only exception is in overlapping to blend colors. Then it is best to place dark wax over light wax. Leaving space in and around the colored waxed shapes permits the dye to become more integrated with the colors and improves the overall design. After waxing is completed, the fabric is squeezed carefully to crack the wax a little. Only one dye is needed. Either it is brushed over the fabric or the fabric is immersed in it. At one time lightweight fabrics were recommended, because the wax should penetrate the fabric. Today all kinds of fabric are used. It is generally easier to batik lighter colored fabrics, but, by all means, experiment. Colored inks can be used as well as dyes. Remove wax from the fabric as in the regular batik process. The hot iron melts the wax out, but the color remains in the fabric. Batik can be done successfully on scrap materials because it is pretty much mistake-proof. Interesting and unexpected effects always occur. That is why it has intrigued people for centuries.

Chapter 7

PAPER AND CARDBOARD

The fabulous array of available papers from delicately thin to velvety velour excites the imagination. Papers might be transparent, translucent or opaque, with surfaces varying from glossy to dull. They can be patterned, gaily colored or neutral. Fadeless and fluorescent papers are appearing in greater numbers and self-adhering papers are more readily available. Plastic finishes on paper with many surfaces washable are excellent for durability and soil resistance. Traditional tan and gray cardboard—pliable to rigid—has taken on a new look with interesting surface decorations. Of all the materials, paper is the easiest to obtain. Most merchants are willing to let you have their paper and cardboard discards, which might be promotional materials, wrappings or packagings. Especially valuable to recyclists are discontinued wallpaper and greeting card sample books. Every home and business accumulates excess or used paper and cardboard at a phenomenal rate. Some of the most common are: newspapers, magazines, circulars, catalogues, telephone books and calendars; bagging and wrapping papers in various grades and sizes; gift wrapping and tissue papers; packagings of all sorts, and tubes in many sizes and weights. In addition, there are greeting cards, stationery, envelopes and used stamps; cardboard produce trays

Fig. 7-1. Patchwork sheeting.

and grilles; milk, cream and juice cartons. There is a continuous supply of waxed, typing and carbon papers; tapes; bread, candy and gum wrappers; road maps; wallpapers; cigar bands and computer cards.

Before throwing away bits of paper you have amassed, consider the possibility of combining them into unusually attractive patchwork paper. Select paper scraps which seem to go together; think about color, texture and quality. Tear or cut them into shapes which have some relationship, or contrast them with good design in mind. There are several ways to attach one piece to another. Holes could be punched on the edges of the paper shapes and yarn or string woven in and out of them as part of the over-all design. The shapes might be overlapped, woven or slit and interlocked, then stitched, taped or glued in place. After the patchwork sheet is assembled, it can be given an individual touch with any art medium. Cardboard may be used. Lightweight cardboard is especially effective.

Fig. 7-2. Glued white paper shapes replace black paper cut-out shapes.

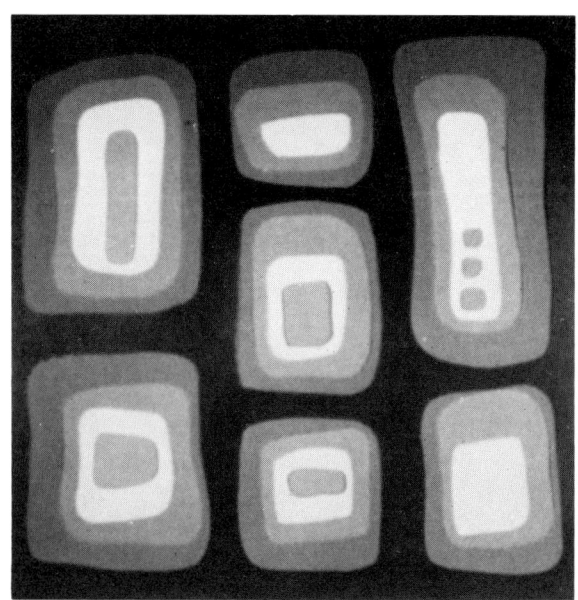

Fig. 7-3. Paper molas.

A variety of papers can be used together with exciting results merely by cutting shapes out of one and replacing them with the same shapes but cut from a different sheet, or sheets, of paper. These shapes can be neatly taped on from the back or the paper can be mounted on a backing and the shapes pasted into position. Accenting with art media may or may not be needed.

We can borrow an idea from the Cuna Indians of the San Blas Islands who make a mola, or blouse, from several layers of differently colored materials superimposed upon each other. Shapes are cut at different levels exposing the several fabrics. This handcraft is so effective we call it the art of molas. Translating it to paper, we start with four or more attractively different pieces about the same size. The paper selected for the bottom is not cut. Some shapes are cut in a second sheet, but not too large at first. They can always be increased in size. This sheet is placed over the first one. This bottom sheet, of course, is seen only through the cut shapes. Cutting shapes is continued in succeeding layers. Each layer has slightly larger cut shapes which are glued over the previous ones. This is a very absorbing activity as you watch the shapes fill with color.

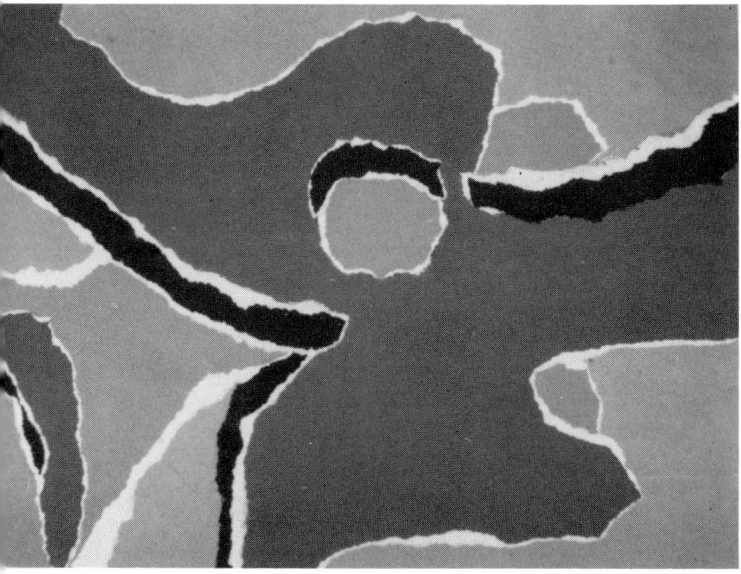

Fig. 7-4. Reverse paper molas.

The same idea can be done in reverse and is especially effective with leftover heavier papers and cardboards. One piece is selected to serve as a base. On it are placed large shapes torn or cut from whatever paper is available. Shapes are gradually made smaller as they are glued upon each other. From the top, the paper shapes somewhat resemble a contour map with different levels of elevation. The layering permits a great deal of imagination to be exercised and results in uninhibited designs.

This idea can be carried a step further if heavy paper or cardboard is used and the number of layers permits printmaking. When the material is quite absorbent, sealing it with diluted white glue, polymer medium, shellac or varnish is required if several prints are to be made. Printing ink is rolled over the relief, tipping the brayer to reach all levels. Thin paper is placed over the inked surface and rubbed with fingers. The print may have an unusually subtle halo effect due to the layering.

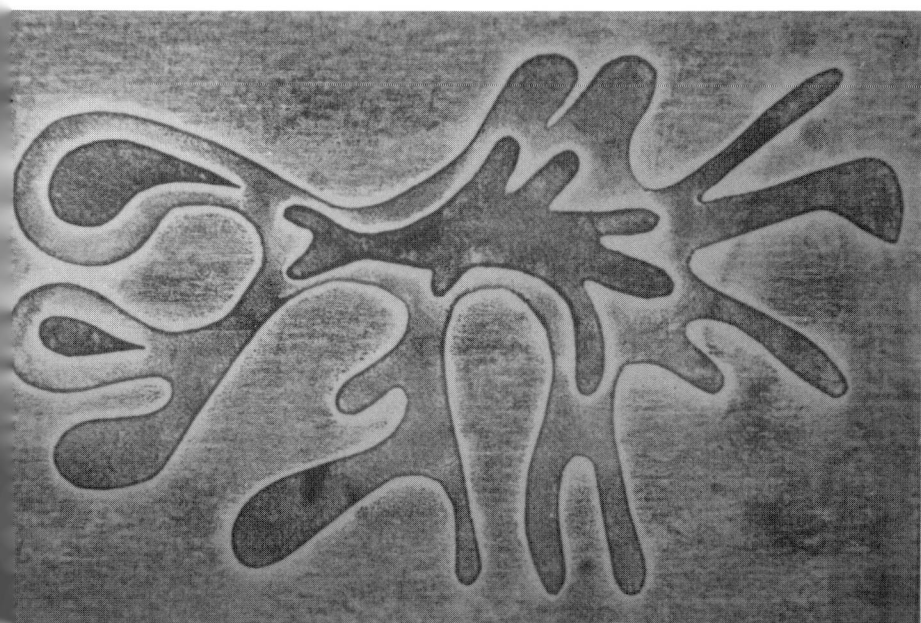

Fig. 7-5. Reverse paper molas printmaking.

Fig. 7-6. Assorted scrap papers.

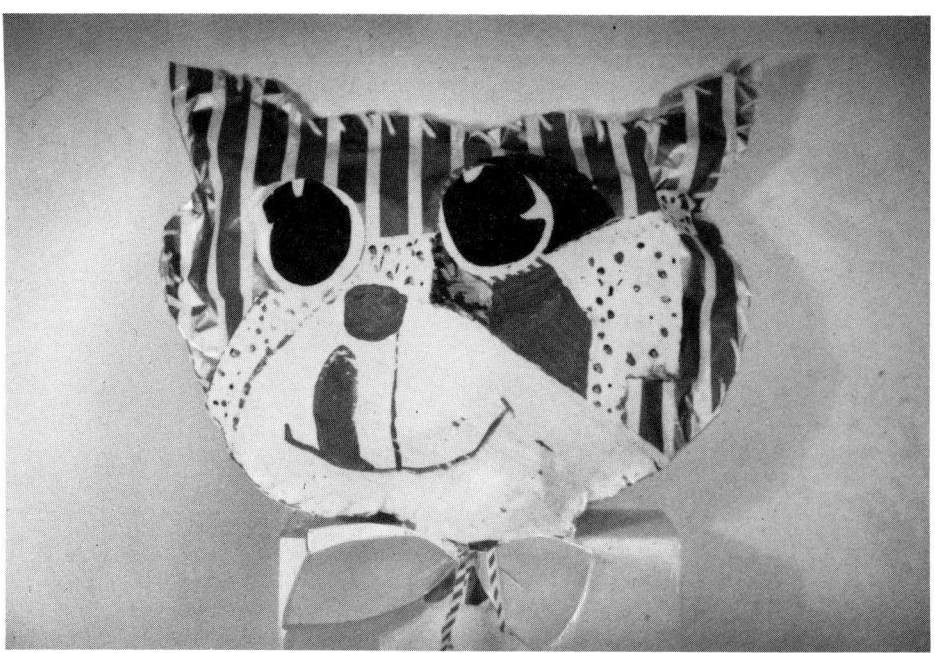

Fig. 7-7. Tempera on wrapping paper.

97

Fig. 7-8. Wrapping paper; yarn; found objects.

Large leftover sheets, such as gift wrapping papers, become three-dimensional forms when stuffed with tissue paper, newspaper, plastic bags or panty hose. If the paper tears too readily, it is lined with heavier paper, such as paper sacking.

Fig. 7-9. Wrapping paper; tailor cardboard.

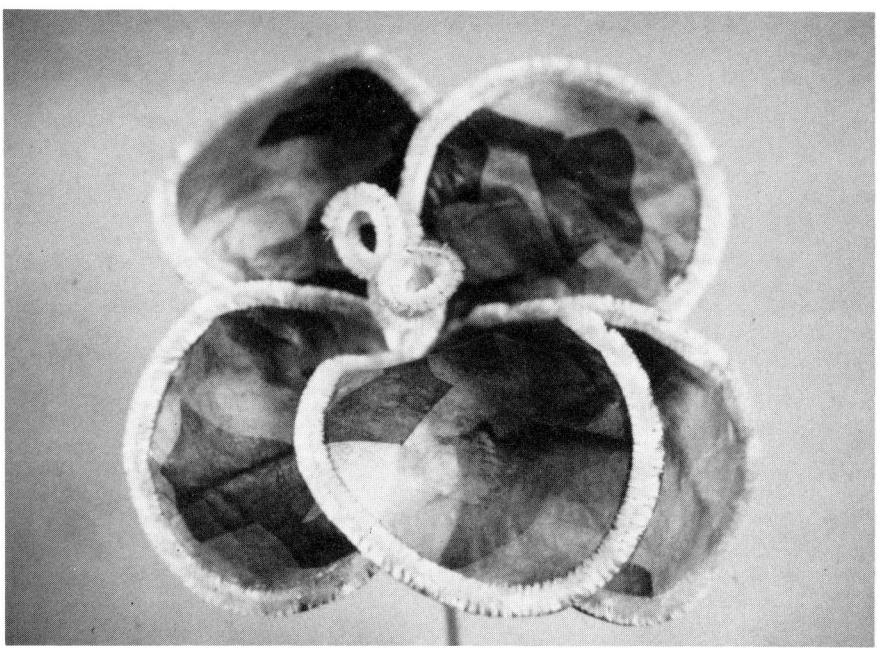

Fig. 7-10. *Laminated tissue paper shaped with pipe cleaners.*

If you wish the paper you are working with were just a bit stronger, held a shape a little better or were just as interesting from the back as from the front, then layering may be the answer. Depending upon the strength needed, two, three or more papers are cut the exact size of the one to be strengthened or shaped. They do not necessarily have to be the very same paper unless the back will be seen and must be the same as the front. Sometimes, soft tissue adds sufficient body. Newspapers may also be used successfully. If there is danger of the black print bleeding through, the reverse side of the top paper is sprayed with aluminum paint. An application of thinned gesso can also serve as a buffer. The layers are sandwiched together with an adhesive. If the papers are to be folded or shaped in any way, it might be best to do it before the glue dries thoroughly.

Spraying with one or two light coats of clear plastic or brushing with a polymer medium seals and gives body to paper. This makes handling and cutting fine

Fig. 7-11. Quilling.

paper easier. Thinned wallpaper paste or wall sizing reinforces heavy paper when applied to the back. Thinned shellac or varnish will seal and stiffen paper, but to avoid excessive absorption and buckling of the paper they must be applied quickly and lightly. Cardboards vary in degrees of absorption; gesso might be needed as an undercoat before applying polymer medium, shellac or varnish. In addition to layering and strengthening, fine wires, pipe cleaners, wooden slats or cardboard may be hidden within the layers or attached to the surface, either concealed or as part of the design.

Arranging rolled strips of paper and attaching them into designs which may or may not be mounted is quilling. Centuries ago people discovered the interesting results possible through this simple process. With the passage of time quilling became more elaborate in Europe and America. Intricate and detailed examples can be found in some museums, old estates and eighteenth century American restorations such as Williamsburg, Virginia. Contemporary taste frowns upon the tight little scrolls of generations past. The modern approach is freer, more colorful and highly individual. Almost anything, such as pencils, square sticks, knitting needles or tongue depressors, are used for rolling the cut or torn paper strips. White glue may be daubed on the rolls or placed in a flat saucer and the edges of the rolls dipped in. Fingers or tweezers are used in placing the coils together. Quilling may be displayed against a contrasting background, in a see-through frame, as a mobile, and, if sturdy enough, it can stand alone. The strips may be embellished as desired, for example, a felt tip pen border on the paper edge. There isn't any reason why the paper strips could not be tapered or other materials incorporated into the design.

Rolling paper gives it a springy quality. When slipped off the object used for rolling it, the paper will spring open into its own shape. The shape of the coil is controlled with fingers. Pinching here and there changes the shape. The end of a strip is glued to its roll, then rolls are combined and glued into a design.

Fig. 7-12. Folded and cut gift wrapping paper.

Ever since paper was invented, folding and cutting it has been a delightful experience. With quick and deft snipping of their shears, the Polish people have turned it into an internationally recognized art form. Folding a piece of paper into a compact little form and cutting out any manner of shapes results, upon opening the paper, in a deceptively intricate design. Its success depends, in part, upon a repetition of the snipping determined by the way the paper is folded. There aren't any hard and fast rules about folding paper. Different foldings give varied results.

Suggested ways of folding paper are:

Any size sheet folded in half; once, twice or three times again;

Any size sheet—fold two parallel edges to meet in the center; crease them; bring the two creased edges together;

Any size sheet can be pleated fan-like in any width;

Any size sheet can be pleated fan-like; then starting at one end fold into squares, rectangles or triangles;

Any size sheet folded in half horizontally; then folded in half vertically;

A square sheet folded in half; in half again to make a square; once or twice again;

A square sheet folded in half; in half again to make a square; once or twice in a triangle;

A square sheet folded diagonally gives a triangular shape; halve the triangle once, twice or three times;

A round sheet folded in half; in half again to make a quarter of a circle shape; fold once or twice more.

Fig. 7-13. Three-dimensional paper sculpture and found objects.

A variation on folded paper is to cut a straight, curved, jagged, wavy or combination line from one folded side in the direction of another folded side, but stopping before completely reaching it. The paper is flipped over. Again a line is cut to the opposite folded side (where the first line started from) stopping before completely reaching it.

The paper is flipped over and cuts repeated any number of times. There will be a series of alternating lines from one folded edge to the other. The folded paper is opened. The alternating cuts have given it an elastic quality and the paper can be stretched within its limits. Cuts can be made from one folded edge without alternating and the results will be different. More complex and involved cuttings reap diverse results. Considering all the folding possibilities with a heap of scrap papers plus a variety of cuts and snips the design potential is really great.

Folding can be used to give a three-dimensional quality to a sheet of paper. Should the paper be somewhat resistant or if cardboard is used, scoring makes a neat crease. To score, determine where the fold is to be. Mark it with a pencil if needed. Press on the line with something that will crease it, but it must not be sharp enough to go through the paper or cardboard surface. Scissor handles, scissor tips, paper clips, dull knives, ball point pens or anything handy that will do the job might be used for scoring.

Fig. 7-14. Sculptured paper.

Fig. 7-15. Sculptured and scored paper.

Fig. 7-16. Paper sculpture.

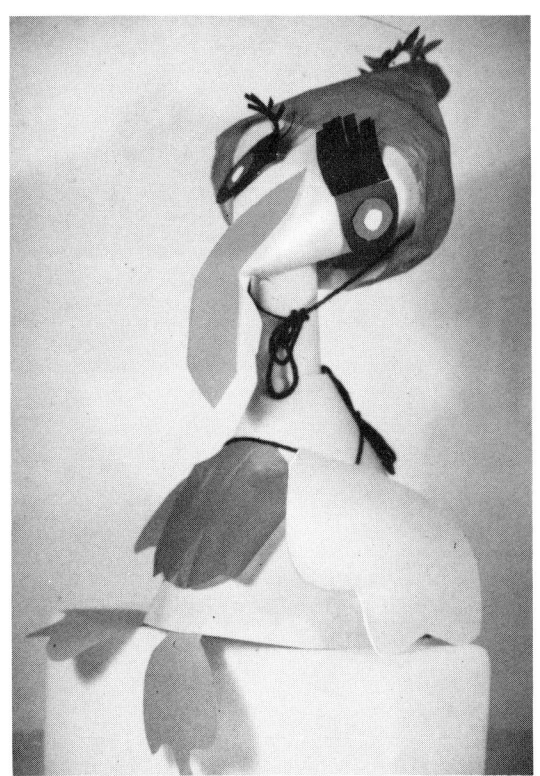

Fig. 7-17. Sculptured paper.

The paper or cardboard you wish to recycle may fall short of your expectations. It may be just too dull in color, too ordinary in appearance or it doesn't quite fit in with what you are doing. You can change its appearance and there are several ways to do so.

If the paper to be changed is absorbent, then dyeing is a speedy and effective way to achieve extraordinary results. Food coloring, colored inks, thinned tempera, heavily pigmented watercolor, dyes or stains can be used. Anything that stains, such as coffee, tea or beet juice, is good, but color selection may be limited. A repeat design can be made if the paper is carefully folded. There are many ways to do this. One way is to pleat the paper (any size pleats will do). Another way is to have two outer edges meet in the center; crease them; then meet creased edges and fold. The size of the paper has been reduced in one direction. It is now a folded strip and must be kept that way. To reduce the size of the paper in the other direction it is folded into squares, triangles or rectangles. Folding is started at one end and continued on the strip. If it comes out uneven when the end is reached, the paper is not cut off. After dyeing, it may be discovered that it was an integral part of the design. The sheet of paper now resembles a compact little square, triangle or rectangle. It is ready for dipping into the dyes.

Bowls of colored dyes will be needed and one bowl of clear water. The strength of the dyes is determined by the color value wanted (tint, middle or shade) and the absorbency of the paper used. The length of time the paper is left in the dye also regulates the depth of the color. One must experiment until satisfied. Only the corners of the folded paper are dipped into the dyes for as long as one pleases. Not every corner need be dipped. Dipping may be deep or shallow. Colors may be varied or all alike and more than one color used in a corner. The clear bowl of water is for dipping a corner when extra color bleeding is desired. Combinations, of course, are many. Excess dye is pressed out between two pieces of cardboard. The paper is unfolded and set aside to dry. No one has ever made just one and stopped! The results are always gratifying and no two are ever alike. To make a random design, the paper is folded in any manner and dipped into the dyes any number of times. The dyes might also be brushed or splattered onto the paper.

Fig. 7-18. Dyed wrapping paper.

Fig. 7-19. Oil pastel design on wallpaper.

Crayons are commonly used for changing the appearance of paper. They are so versatile it seems unnecessary to say much about them. They are wax and oil based and fluorescents increase their large selection of colors. There are wax and oil colored pencils, too. Crayons when applied heavily resist water based liquids. Art forms where they are used together are called Crayon Resists. If detergent is added to the liquid, the resistance is lessened. Heavy applications of crayon can be covered with this kind of mixture and scratched through to reveal the crayon; this is Crayon Etch. Wax crayons can be held at the base of a candle flame (to avoid blackening) and dripped on paper and cardboard. If melted over hot water and painted on, the process is known as encaustic painting. When used on their sides, crayons give quick coverage. If a thin to medium paper is placed over a textured surface and a crayon rubbed over the paper, an imprint of the texture is immediately made.

There are other dry media to use on paper. Pastel is a better grade of chalk; charcoal can be very much like chalk; all are powdery. To reduce dust, the paper or cardboard is dampened before applying the medium or the medium is dipped into a little sugar water, buttermilk or milk with vinegar, and used on a dry surface. Generally more subtle than crayons, these dry materials may be blended with fingers, tissues, crumpled or left as is. When a thin or medium paper is placed over a textured surface and chalk rubbed over the paper, the results can be quite delicate. Pastel and charcoal papers have "tooth" or special textures, which mean that the fine particles of pastel, chalk and charcoal have somewhere to settle. They are not compatible with slick papers. Often the delicacy is lessened and the color darkened by spraying with a fixative after using these dry materials.

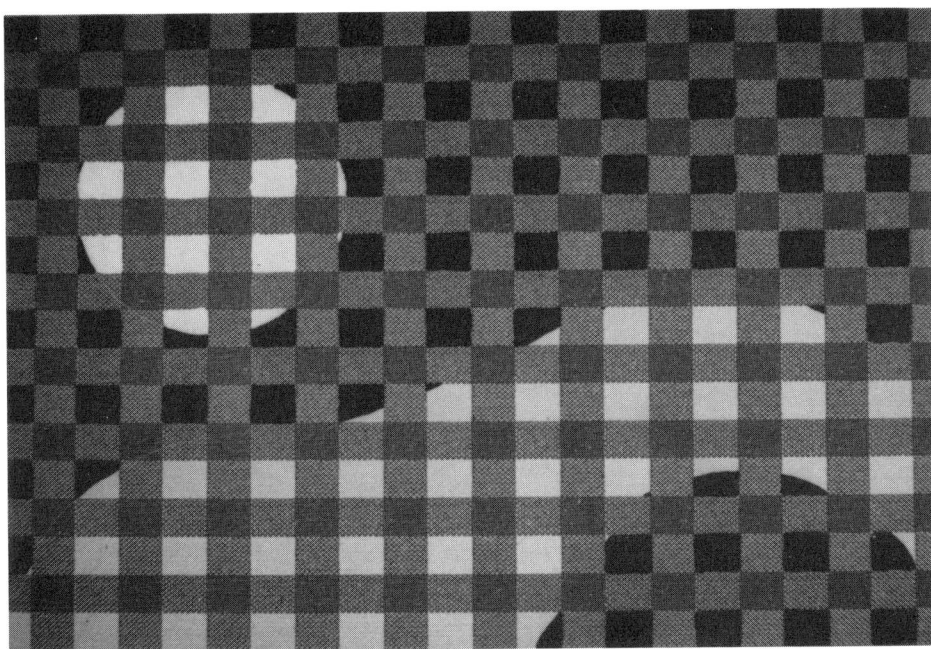

Fig. 7-20. Tempera painted checked wallpaper (sample book).

Paper and cardboard accept practically all paints. Surfaces treated with tough resistant coatings, wallpapers in particular, often repel paint. Some paints are more compatible with surfaces made expressly for them, such as watercolor on watercolor paper. Manufacturers offer many kinds of paint applied in any manner from fingers to sprays in every imaginable color plus the fluorescents and phosphorescents.

One need not fear messy clean-ups any more; modern technology has made painting a pleasure from beginning to end. Luminous, transparent and miscible colored inks applied to paper are long standing favorites. They are ideal for accenting, washes and delicate renderings. Waterproof black India ink can be thinned with water for gray tints. Extremely versatile, clean and easy to use water and waterproof felt tip pens have become very popular. Their artistic value is high and they are excellent for use on paper and cardboard.

Fig. 7-21. Acrylic painted shopping bag.

Fig. 7-22. Tempera painted cardboard.

The surface of any paper or cardboard can be quickly transformed with printmaking. Find an appealingly textured surface, a provocative form, or incise a design. Spread the surface evenly with color; a brayer and block printing inks work easily. Lay the paper on the colored surface and rub. Be sure you are getting a good print. Lift the paper and there you have it! All manner and means of transferring color and design from one surface to another have been devised; they all work well on paper and cardboard.

Fig. 7-23. Inked shirt cardboard.

Fig. 7-24. Textured bagging.

We think of paper and cardboard as being relatively smooth or somewhat textured. Crumpling paper in our hand and smoothing it out creates interesting surface texture. Discover the effects that are likely with art materials applied to crumpled paper. Cuts can be made in paper with a scissor or knife and lifted or curled up to form a textured surface. The smooth top layer of corrugated cardboard can be pulled away in areas revealing the textural linear quality of the corrugation. There are times when destroying parts of a surface is the best thing to do: punching and tearing holes, slashing into strips and charring edges and holes. Then there is camouflage: altering a surface, in part or whole, by attaching any number of materials, such as flock, sparkle, sand, sequins, tapes, ribbons and laces.

Fig. 7-25. Magazine textured collage.

Before newspapers and magazines are disposed of it takes but a few minutes to check for art articles of interest to share with others through bulletin boards or collections. We tend to overlook newspapers as a design source. Not all pages are suitable, of course, but many do make excellent backgrounds for drawing, painting, printmaking and collage. Pages with long, even columns, such as telephone directories, when turned sidewards, make good practice sheets for learning brush control in lettering. Newspapers, because they are readily available and cheap, can be used to test ideas and plan original designs with a big brush and tempera, felt tip markers or by cutting out shapes. When tightly rolled on the diagonal and taped, they are useful in building paper structures limited only by the imagination. Cutting out and combining in new ways the lettering, simulated textures, colors and designs found in printed matter creates collages and comic pictures. After gluing, polymer mediums, diluted white glue or shellac may be brushed on for a finishing touch.

Fig. 7-26. Scrap papers sculptured into shapes; inked.

Fig. 7-27. Moulage.

To the French *moulage* means to "mold a shape," and there are many ways to mold paper. Through experimenting one generally finds a personal preference. A picture or design is made and studied carefully to determine what part or parts are to stand out in relief. They are traced and transferred to a piece of paper and colored as in the picture or design. Cardboard strip supports are glued on the back of the cut-out shapes to raise them above the original drawing. Cut-outs may extend any distance. They may be at the same or different levels. When dried, they are glued in position on the picture or design. With some shapes the relief effect is enhanced by contouring the edges of the cut pieces. The cut piece is placed face down in the palm of a slightly cupped hand. With the side of a small round pencil the edges of the piece are gently pressed in an outward motion.

Instead of cardboard strips to make the shapes stand out, more flexible materials can be used such as papier mâché, pulp, bread formula, modeling compound or clear silicone seal. Where a shape is to be positioned, one of the many moldable materials is placed and the shape is rounded and sculptured over it. Excess materials which may extend beyond the paper shape can easily be removed with a damp sponge. The cut shape is contoured with the palm of the hand before placing on the mound of moldable material. It is possible to build one shape on top of another with just a small glob of silicone seal. This material remains pliable when dry, making layering of shapes feasible. It may be necessary to mount the picture or design for support if much paper molding is done. Seal with polymer medium, shellac or varnish for added permanence.

Chapter 8
PLASTICS

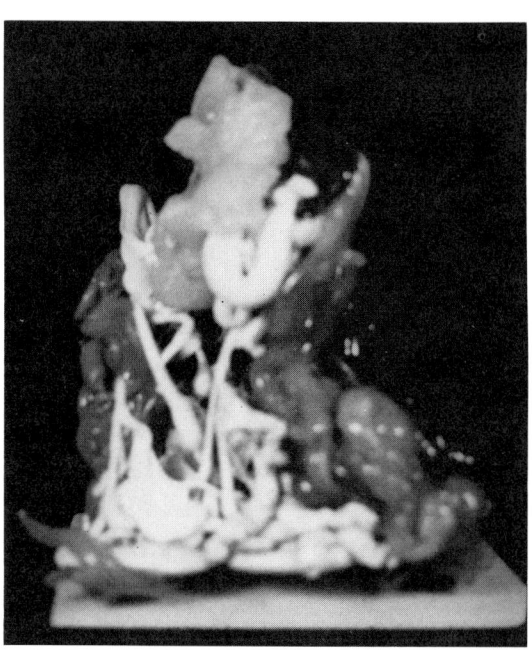

Fig. 8-1. Extruded plastic scrap.

One need not worry about finding scrap plastic; there is an overabundance. This technological discovery of the twentieth century has made a dramatic impact on our lives. Light in weight, inexpensive, versatile and quite indestructible (within certain limits): these qualities contribute to its widespread use. Although plastics can be made to simulate other materials, they are individually exciting in their own way. Properties differ radically among them and there always lurks the element of surprise in working with discarded plastics.

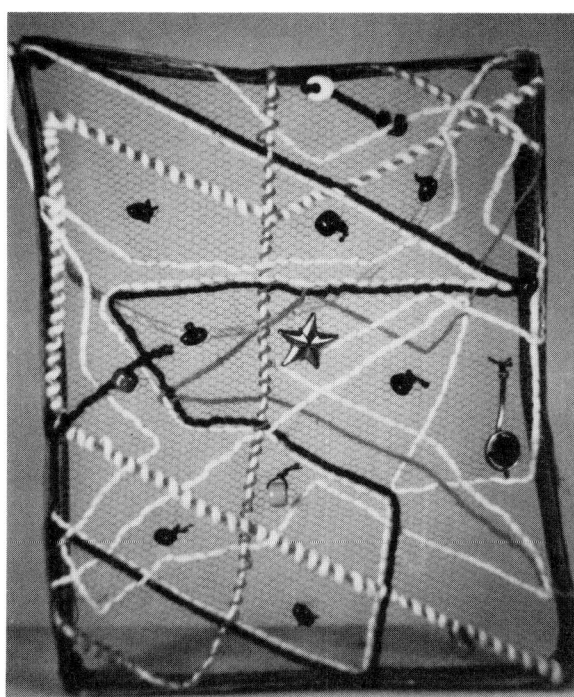

Fig. 8-2. Plastic netting and keepsakes.

Fig. 8-4. Yellow net turkey bag woven with yarn and wooden beads.

Many items are sold in colorful plastic nettings which are suitable for weaving and collage.

Fig. 8-3. Plastic mesh with seashore theme.

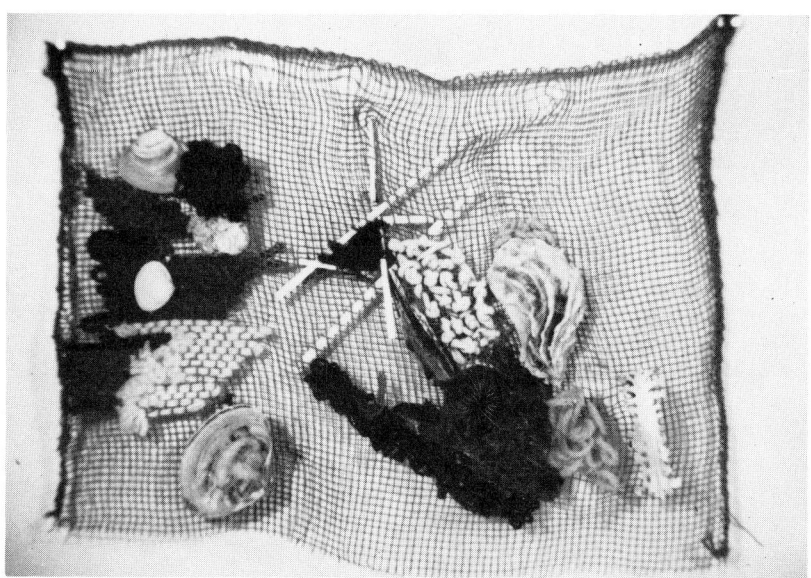

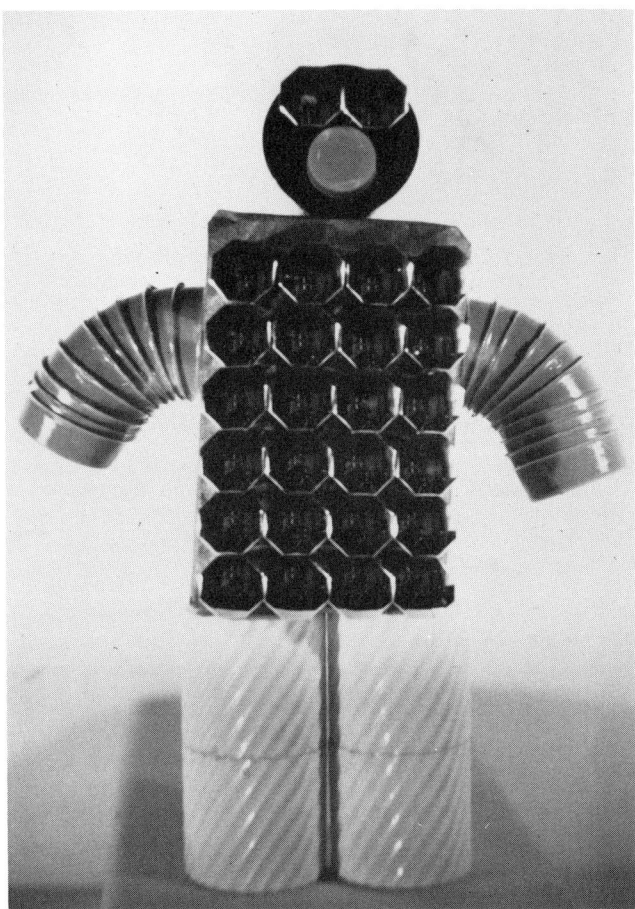

Fig. 8-5. Plastic scrap pieces joined with white glue.

Successfully adhering together an odd assortment of plastic materials, as in Figs. 8-5 through 8-7, depends upon the chemical composition of the parts and the strain the joined sections must undergo. There are plastics that resist some glues. Others are eaten away by certain bonding agents. The characteristics of a plastic are not always visually apparent. A rule of thumb would be to use a white glue first. If unsuccessful, try an epoxy. If the use warrants buying plastic adhesives, check the manufacturers' labels to see which suits your particular needs.

Making holes to tie plastic pieces together sometimes requires heat. Depending upon the size of the holes needed, heat a large needle, sharp nail, ice pick, awl or pointed knife until very hot over a burner or at the base of a candle flame (prevents the tool from getting sooty and discoloring the plastic). Pliers can be used to hold an instrument without a handle. Insert the hot sharp point into the plastic with a quick in and out motion. This may have to be repeated a few times. Nylon fishing line is good for tying parts together.

113

Fig. 8-6. Assorted items tied or glued.

Fig. 8-7. Plastic cup hat; plastic excelsior and findings; glued.

Fig. 8-8. *Polystyrene trays; permanent felt tip markers.*

Much of the merchandise we buy is sold in transparent, translucent or opaque plastic packaging with varying degrees of flexibility. Nonabsorbent white plastic foam produce trays are brittle and crack when too much pressure is applied. Water based liquids mixed with a detergent, oil paints and acrylics are used for painting them. Permanant felt tip markers are excellent for coloring and texturing the surface. Many solvents dissolve the plastic, but with control they can create interesting surface changes. The picture of the little house in Fig. 8-8 shows how the natural contours of the trays can be used to advantage. Masking tape and white glue hold the pieces together.

115

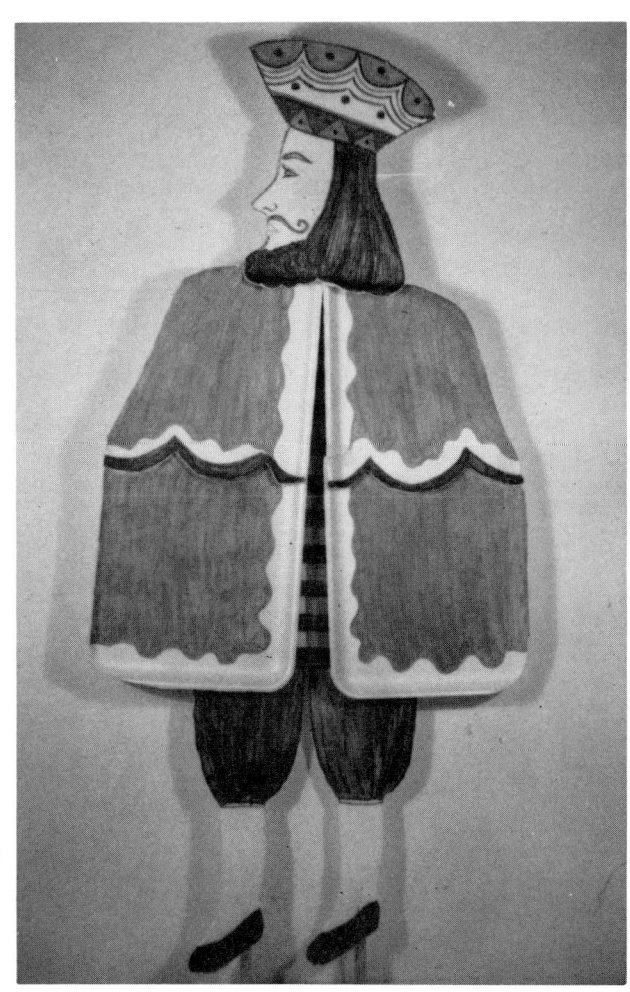

Fig. 8-9. Plastic trays; tempera plus detergent.

Much thought went into creating the king. The trays were cut with scissors to use the contours in the right places, as the ends of his beard and hair and at the bottom of his cloak. Edges were sanded where needed. Two tongue depressors stuck into a white foam base are his support.

Fig. 8-10. Plastic trays; permanent felt tip pens.

The animal creature, the lady bunny and the fanciful bird are happy and uniquely individual expressions. Do not overlook the potential in plastic produce trays which can be easily dented. For example, a design may be impressed by applying medium pressure with a pencil eraser. The tray surface can then be used as a block printing master or, simply, a relief design.

117

Fig. 8-11. Plastic trays; cardboard hat; acrylics.

Fig. 8-12. Polyurethane trays; tissue paper; permanent markers.

Fig. 8-13. Plastic trays and egg cartons; permanent felt tip pens; white glue.

Cardboard egg cartons are being replaced in several localities with pastel colored plastic cartons. The material resembles plastic produce trays and can be handled similarly. In fact, combinations of the two provide unlimited possibilities. This type of plastic, when placed in hot water near the boiling point, quickly becomes pliable and can be curled and molded into different forms. This takes a little experimenting. Pliers may be used to bend and twist the plastic. Use caution, because the surface is easily marred. Using protective gloves and a light touch you can also mold the plastic. You might care to try this technique for changing the form of a piece of plastic with other plastic materials. If a plastic is classified as thermoplastic, it will become soft and sufficiently heated and harden into whatever form you have created. It is not always possible to recognize whether a plastic has this property. This is one way to determine its plasticity.

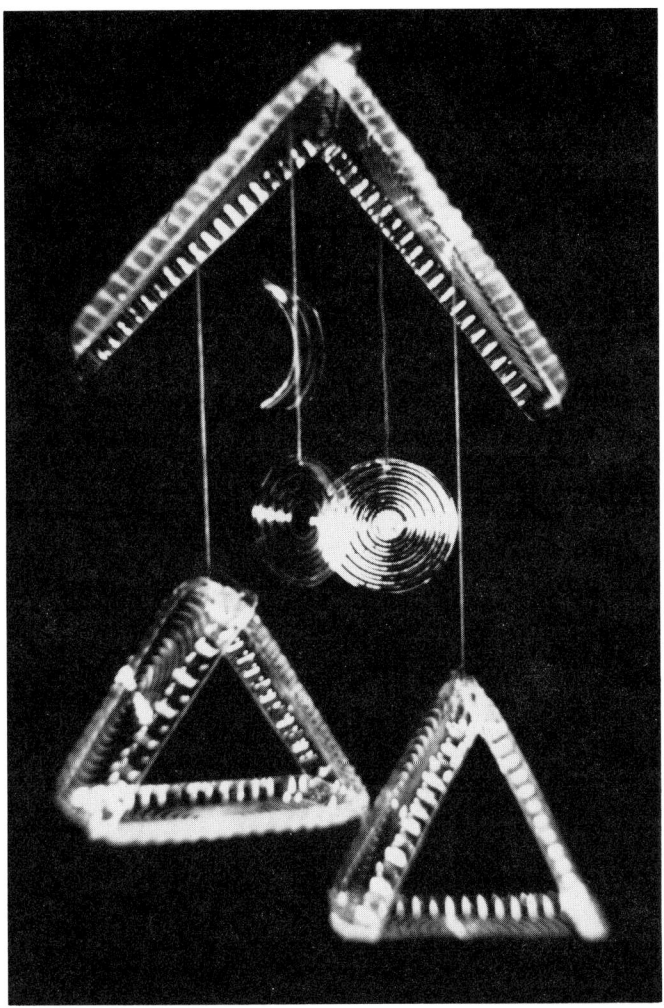

Fig. 8-14. Transparent plastic.

Fig. 8-15. Colored plastic shot and yarn glued on sheetrock.

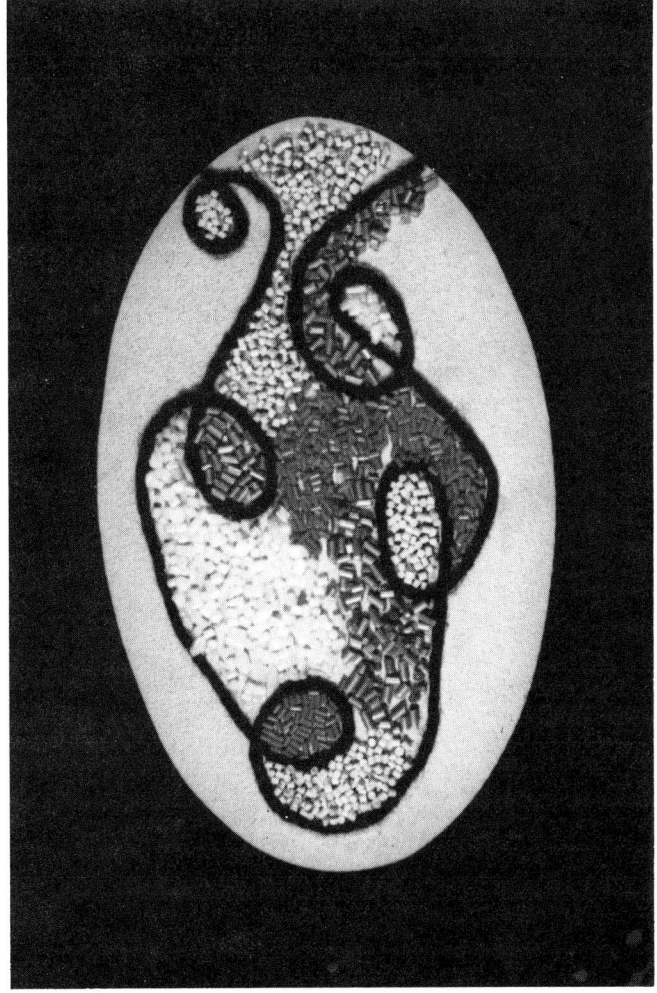

Experimenting with stains, dyes, paints, sprays, solvents, lacquers, shellacs, varnishes, heat and light on different kinds of plastic is stimulating. Surprisingly, thin transparent plastic becomes delicately frosted with clear plastic spray and translucent plastic seems transparent when lacquer or varnish is applied to both sides of it. They may be tinted before applying. Explore the possibilities in squeezable, white and pastel plastic pellets and tiny, colorful plastic shot which are used to protect commodities in shipments. Recyclists are constantly alerted to the new uses industry finds for plastics.

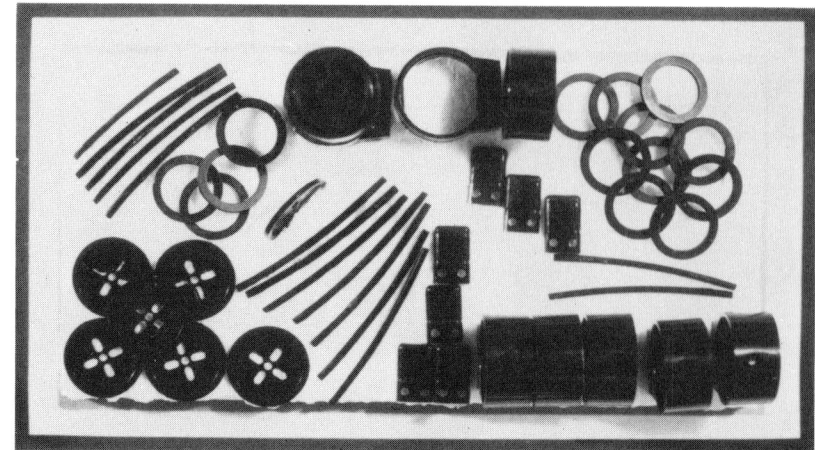

Fig. 8-16. *Government surplus; white glue; cardboard mounting.*

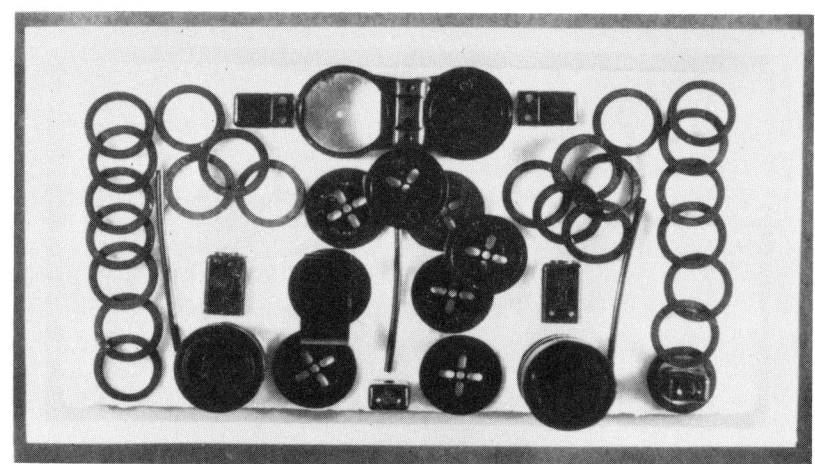

Fig. 8-17. *Government surplus; white glue; cardboard mounting.*

With emphasis on composition and movement, an art teacher had a fourth-grade class mount a variety of discarded similar plastic forms.

Fig. 8-18. *Government surplus; white glue; cardboard mounting.*

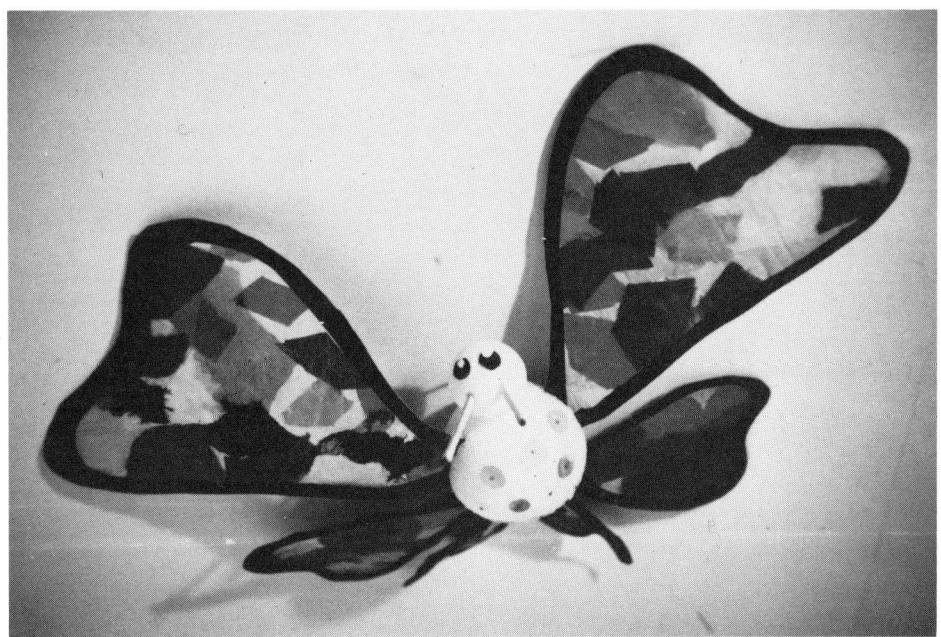

Fig. 8-19. Styrofoam balls with attached wings and appendages; sequins; food coloring.

The plastic most familiar, perhaps, is styrofoam; it is often used for holiday decorations. This is a polystyrene but of a different density than a plastic produce tray. Styrofoam might be characterized as being "crunchy." Materials can be adhered to its surface with pins which do not noticeably mar its porosity. Although it is an enduring material, it must be protected from abrasion. The size of the scrap piece of styrofoam determines how best to form it. Serrated knife blades or saws work well for cutting. Sandpapers, rasps, rifflers and files are effective, too. With control, turpentine and acetone, among other solvents, are used to pit the surface. Another way to change the texture is to cause spot burning by applying a steady flame or subjecting the piece to intense heat. This can be most effective, but use adequate ventilation because the fumes are considered toxic. Cutting lines can be marked on styrofoam with a china marking or grease pencil. Be certain that the paint you use is compatible with styrofoam, otherwise, your work of art might disintegrate before your very eyes.

Fig. 8-20. Polystyrene; cellophane; acrylics.

Fig. 8-21. Polyurethane; oils; fish line.

Fig. 8-22. Plastic produce trays; tempera and detergent; polymer medium.

Scraps of acrylic sheeting—you may recognize this as Lucite or Plexiglas—may have gummed protective paper attached. This is handy for sketching your design but more important, it prevents marring the surface. Do not remove the protective paper until absolutely necessary. This is a wonderful material to work with and woodworking tools may be used. Should a lubricant be needed, soap and water are satisfactory. If your scrap is heated (about 250°F), it will become very pliable and can be curved or bent into another form. Before reaching the ignition point of about 700°F the material will undergo changes. All this may be to an advantage if one wishes to experiment. There are special bonding agents which soften the acrylic to make joints that harden clear. Epoxy, neatly applied, can be used to attach acrylic parts or to adhere other substances. Transparent, translucent, colored, textured and patterned plastic panels are popularly used in exterior and interior remodeling. If you find this kind of scrap you will derive much pleasure translating it into art forms.

Rarely does one's imagination falter when working with plastics. In Figs. 8-20 through 8-24 plastics took different directions as individuals became thoroughly involved with the medium.

Fig. 8-23. White plastic sheeting; permanent press fabric; felt; yarn.

Fig. 8-24. Plastic covers; pins; balsa wood; cardboard base; spray paint.

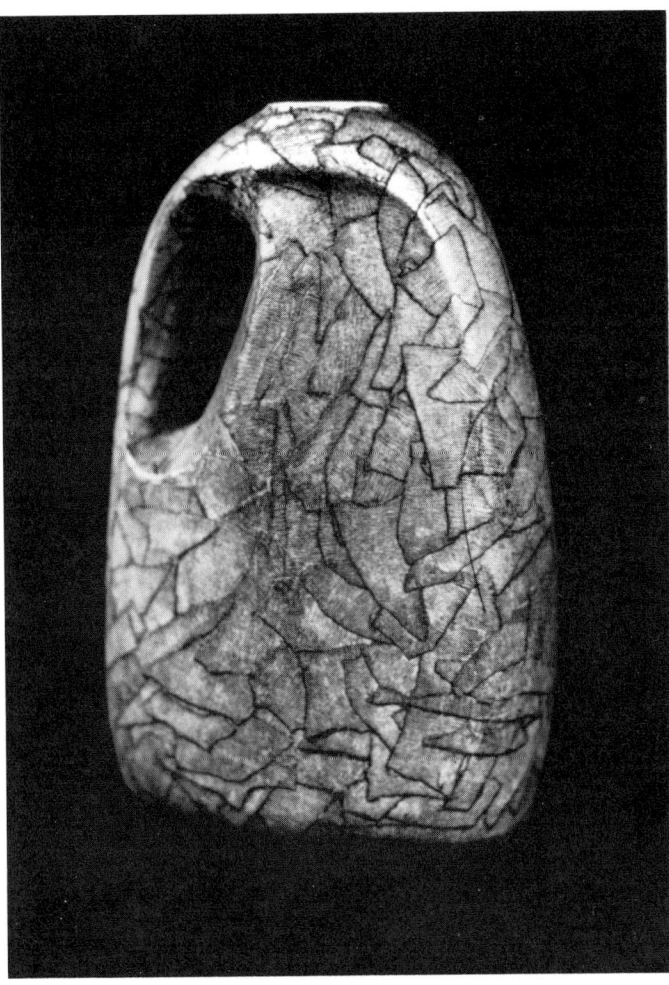

Fig. 8-25. Plastic container; masking tape; shoe polish.

If you find a well-designed plastic form, many changes can be made to its surface. In Fig. 8-25 the threaded part was cut from a half gallon detergent bottle. Its surface was covered with torn pieces of masking tape and shoe polish was rubbed over the bottle. These are equally attractive finishes: pieces from colored magazine sheets and orange shellac, tissue paper shapes and tinted polymer medium, white glue squeezed from its bottle in a linear design and allowed to dry, or partially dry, then acrylic painted in any manner.

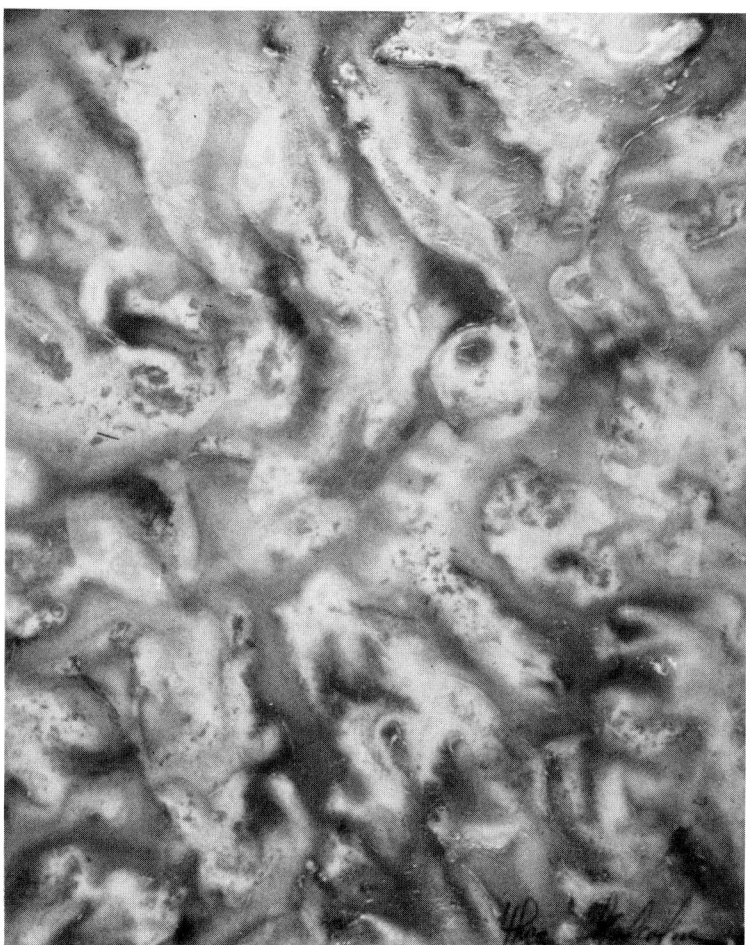

Fig. 8-26. White glue and water colors on gesso panel.

Don't dispose of half-empty bottle of plastic-based white glue. It is impossible to duplicate a lovely nonobjective painting made with white glue poured at random over a sturdy support. The glue will slowly begin to spread out; it is not necessary to cover the entire surface. Protect the areas around the picture with newspapers until control is mastered. Drip water colors, colored inks or thinned acrylic paints into the glue. The painting becomes "alive" as the glue and colors create movement. This is a most fascinating experience well worth trying.

ACKNOWLEDGMENTS

I want to extend my sincere appreciation to Mrs. Pat Trotter, art specialist, and Mr. Roy A. Egatz, principal, of the Woodside Avenue School in Franklin Lakes, New Jersey, for "Animal Fantasy," and Mrs. Michele Tilli, art specialist, and Mr. C. Hunziker, principal, of the Theunis Dey School in Wayne, New Jersey, for the totems. My thanks also go to Mr. Frank Manning, Mr. Frank Capasso, Mrs. Jeanne Alvine and Mrs. Lois Suarez of the Pequannock Township High School in Pompton Plains, New Jersey; Mrs. Caroline McGuigan, art teacher, at the Stephen J. Gerace School in Pequannock, New Jersey; Mrs. Ethel Salman and Mr. Robert Gutmann of the art department in the Dumont, New Jersey, High School; Mr. Basil Fattel and Mr. Stephen Kayne of the Paterson, New Jersey, Public Schools; Mrs. Renee De John, art specialist, in the Wayne, New Jersey, Public Schools; Miss Sarita Rainey, art supervisor, of the West Hartford, Connecticut, Public Schools. They graciously gave me their time and their work. I only wish I could have used all of their student work in recycled art that was available to me, but a book is only just so big! Thanks are extended to the students represented from my own collection which covers a period of years.

I wish to acknowledge the special help these people gave me: Arlene Albalah, Andrew Benincaso, Theodore Beresky, Robert Bradley, Katie Brown, Patti Cameron, Kathy Campbell, Elaine Caracozzo, Terri Decker, Lois Dyksen, Susan Edwards, Olga Gonzalez, Lorraine Gogolen, Peggy Hogan, Sophia Jones, Rosemarie Kelling, Dorothy Lo Cascio, Linda Lovenberg, Linda MacElroy, Dan Martin, Carol McDermott, Lillie Moore, Patty O'Connor, Michele Petillo, Diane Sarnecky, Cindy Shepherd, Terri Short, Karen Spincola, Gail Whitenour, my family, colleagues and friends who offered suggestions and gave encouragement.

BIBLIOGRAPHY

Andrews, Michael F. *Sculpture and Ideas.* Englewood Cliffs: Prentice Hall, Inc. 1966.

Birrell, Verla. *The Textile Arts.* New York: Harper & Brothers, Publishers. 1959.

Coleman, Ronald L. *Sculpture: a Basic Handbook for Students.* Dubuque: Wm. C. Brown Company, Publishers. 1968.

Fabri, Ralph. *Sculpture in Paper.* New York: Watson-Guptill Publications. 1966.

Horn, George F. *Art for Today's Schools.* Worcester: Davis Publications, Inc. 1967.

Jensen, Lawrence N. *Synthetic Painting Media.* Englewood Cliffs: Prentice Hall, Inc. 1964.

Johnstone, James B. *Woodcarving.* Menlo Park: Lane Books. 1971.

Manning, Frank. *Creative Chipcarving.* Pompton Plains, New Jersey: Pequannock Township High School. 1974.

Martin, Charles J. and Victor D'Amico. *How to Make Modern Jewelry.* New York: Doubleday & Company, Inc. The Museum of Modern Art. 1960.

Mattil, Edward L. *Meaning in Crafts.* Englewood Cliffs: Prentice-Hall, Inc. 1971.

Moseley, Spencer, Pauline Johnson and Hazel Koenig. *Crafts Design.* Belmont: Wadsworth Publishing Company, Inc. 1962.

Newman, Thelma R. *Leather as Art and Craft.* New York: Crown Publishers. 1971.

Pattemore, Arnel W. *Printmaking Activities for the Classroom.* Worcester: Davis Publications, Inc. 1966.

Percy, H. M. *New Materials in Sculpture.* London: Alex Tiranti. 1962.

Rainey, Sarita R. *Wall Hangings: Designing with Fabric and Thread.* Worcester:Davis Publications, Inc. 1971.

Rothenberg, Polly. *Creative Stained Glass.* New York: Crown Publishers. 1971.

Rottger, Ernst. *Creative Paper Design.* New York: Reinhold Publishing Corporation. 1963.

Roukes, Nicholas. *Sculpture in Plastics.* New York: Watson-Guptill Publications. 1968.

Savage, John H. *The Practical Handbook of Furniture Refinishing, Restyling and Repair.* New York: Fawcett Publications, Inc. 1971.

Stevens, Harold. *Ways with Art.* New York: Reinhold Publishing Corporation. 1963.

SOUTHEASTERN MASSACHUSETTS UNIVERSITY
TT157.M347
Art from recycled materials

3 2922 00190 786 1

DATE DUE	
OCT 13 1981 RETURNED	FEB 25 1990
JUL 02 1990	FEB 18 1998
AUG 06 1990	DEC 3 - 2003
JUN 28 1993	MAY 31 2004
JUN 30 1993	MAY 13 2004
DEC 28 1994	NOV 17 2006
DEC 30 1994	
NOV 02 1996	
OCT 25 1996	
ILL 2301 9476	OCT 30 2006

261-2500